AQA BUSINESS STUDIES for A2

REVISION GUIDE SECOND EDITION

Ian Marcousé
Naomi Birchall
Claire Marcousé

HODDER
EDUCATION
AN HACHETTE UK COMPANY

Orders: please contact Bookpoint Ltd, 130 Milton Park, Abingdon, Oxon OX14 4SB.
Telephone: (44) 01235 827720. Fax: (44) 01235 400454. Lines are open from 9.00–5.00,
Monday to Saturday, with a 24 hour message answering service. You can also order through
our website www.hoddereducation.co.uk

If you have any comments to make about this, or any of our other titles, please send them
to educationenquiries@hodder.co.uk

British Library Cataloguing in Publication Data
A catalogue record for this title is available from the British Library

ISBN: 978 1 444 10796 8

First Edition Published 2005
This Edition Published 2010
Impression number   10 9 8 7 6 5 4 3 2 1
Year   2014 2013 2012 2011 2010

Hachette UK's policy is to use papers that are natural, renewable and
recyclable products and made from wood grown in sustainable forests.
The logging and manufacturing processes are expected to conform to the
environmental regulations of the country of origin.

Cover illustration © Oxford Illustrators and Designers
Typeset by Phoenix Photosetting, Chatham, Kent
Printed in Italy for Hodder Education, an Hachette UK Company, 338 Euston Road, London
NW1 3BH

Contents

Introduction

This revision book is written to help push every reader's A2 results up by at least one grade. It does this by focusing the subject content on the exam skills sought by examiners. The writing style is analytic, but applied to the context of real businesses, just as the examiners want. Every chapter points out key evaluative themes within the syllabus. As knowledge of the syllabus counts for only one-fifth of the marks at A2 level, revision must do more than re-hash facts and definitions. This Revision Guide teaches the reader to develop all the exam skills needed for success, but with a particular focus on application.

Each Unit within the book covers a different section of the A2 specification. All the key concepts are explained, with the more difficult ones getting longer, fuller explanations. The content is full of references to real firms and application is further enhanced by dedicated sections in the Units. There are also questions to test yourself in every Unit. The answers are set out at the back of the book to provide immediate feedback on how your revision is going.

There are two other features to help build grades:
● At the end of each section (Marketing, Finance and so on) is a final unit containing many questions, including exam-style papers; again, answers are at the back to help you study for yourself
● At the back of the book are Revision Checklists to prompt you to consider carefully whether you know everything you should

In addition to this book, it is hugely helpful to:
● Use the actual and 'specimen' exam papers available at **www.aqa.com**
● Go through the specification content, word by word, using the *A-Z Business Studies Handbook*, Philip Allan 2009 as your companion. This book will be invaluable for your A2 studies and is widely used by 1st year university students – so your money will not be wasted
● Regularly read articles from *Business Review* magazine. It will be available in your school/college library. Look out especially for articles by Andrew Gillespie, Ian Marcousé and Malcolm Surridge.

The Authors

Ian Marcousé has devised the format of the book and edited all the text and questions. Ian was the AS/A2 Chief Examiner for AQA Business Studies for 11 years and remains a leading author. He is also the founding editor of *Business Review* magazine and an active classroom teacher.

Naomi Birchall is an experienced teacher and examiner who now works full time as a writer and an educational consultant. She writes regularly for *Business Review* magazine.

Claire Marcousé achieved her A grade in AQA Business Studies, studied Business and Japanese at Cardiff University and now teaches Business and Economics (and Japanese, when possible). She teaches at Bellerby's College, Greenwich.

1 Corporate objectives and strategies

 **Unit 1** **Corporate objectives and strategies**

What?

A corporate objective is a company-wide goal that must be achieved in order for a firm to reach its overall aim. Whereas an aim is a statement of general intent, an objective should be SMART, that is:

Specific – i.e. precise.

Measurable – there must be a way to measure whether or not the objective has been met.

Ambitious – challenging for the firm to achieve.

Realistic – possible to achieve in the current climate.

Time bound – a time by which the objective must be achieved should be stated.

An example of a SMART objective is:

'To increase net profit from £500m per annum to £600m per annum in the next financial year.'

A corporate strategy is a detailed medium to long-term plan for meeting the corporate objectives.

Why?

Without objectives it may be unclear to middle-management and staff exactly what they are aiming to achieve. Having clear and defined objectives can give employees focus and potentially the motivation to achieve those goals. Who revises harder? The student who hopes to do as well as they can? Or the one who *has* to achieve an A* to get into medical school? Objectives also enable management to measure success. This is important because good businesses are always learning how to get better. Meeting – or failing to meet – an objective can give pause for thought about what went right or wrong.

Objectives are just words, though, without the strategies that make things happen. They set out the actions that need to be taken in order for the organisation to achieve its goals. It is important to see strategy as having two distinct parts:

- The thinking process (which may involve market research or other forms of quantified analysis).
- The doing process, i.e. making the strategy happen.

Some managers are great at the thinking, but weak at executing the ideas (perhaps because their people-management skills are weak). Others have the opposite skill. Needless to say, the star manager is the one who has both.

Which?

Survival

At the start-up stage of business, the key objective will often be survival. In order to achieve this the business will need to grow and make a profit but the fundamental objective is to remain in the market.

During tough economic times, even large organisations may come back to this basic objective. Survival usually relates to the business's finances – without enough cash to pay its short-term debts, a firm cannot survive for long. Therefore strategies related to survival will often relate to the generation or speeding up of cash inflows or the minimisation or delay of cash outflows.

Profit

All profit-making businesses aim to make a profit in the long term. Without profit, it is impossible to grow and – in effect – impossible even to survive. Yet this does not necessarily mean that the key objective at one point in time is profit. Some businesses will be willing to forego short-term profits in order to grow, with the expectation that this will, in the long term, result in increased profit. Others want profit, but not necessarily maximised profits. They may be happy to take a reasonable profit while simultaneously achieving another goal, e.g. a farmer determined to only produce food organically.

For firms that wish to boost profit, there are many possible strategies:

- **Reduce variable cost per unit** – perhaps by switching to low-cost Far Eastern suppliers.
- **Reduce fixed costs** – perhaps by transferring backroom office functions to India.
- **Increase productivity** – perhaps by automating a production function, making some staff redundant.
- **Increase prices** – especially if the product is price inelastic.

Growth

Increasing the size of the firm is often the fundamental objective of established organisations. Growth has the following benefits:

● Increased potential for benefiting from economies of scale – thus enabling costs to be cut. This will enable a firm to make higher profit margins (if the objective is profit) or reduce price in order to increase competitiveness (if the objective is growth).
● Growth often leads to an increase in brand awareness. The larger the organisation the more aware customers will be of its existence.
● Growth in terms of product range or number of stores reduces dependency on key stores or product lines thus spreading risk.
● Especially in the early years of a new product's life cycle, there is often a feeling that unless the business has a large market share, it may get squeezed out of the market by others. Therefore, if the market is growing fast, the firm feels it must grow at least as fast. In this situation, the growth objective is part of a desire for survival.

Diversification

Although diversification could be said to be a form of growth, it is often considered to be an objective in its own right. Diversification is the process of entering a new market with a new product. It can reduce dependence on particular products and therefore, if successful, enables risks to be spread. However, although the aim of diversification is to reduce risk, it is actually a risky objective as entering a relatively unknown market with a new product has a low success rate.

Corporate strategy

A strategy is a medium to long-term plan designed to achieve the business's corporate objectives. It sets out what activities need to be done, when each must be done by and (in some cases) who is responsible for carrying out each activity or ensuring it is carried out.

Corporate strategies in themselves are not tasks, but plans that will have a significant effect on the entire organisation. For example, merging with a competitor, re-focusing on the core products or moving into an international market.

Successful corporate strategies

If a strategy is to succeed, the firm must ensure that it fits with both its strengths and the current environment in which it is operating.

Application

Waitrose is a supermarket chain known and used for its quality not for its price. In 2008 it had to watch its sales falter as shoppers switched to the cheaper supermarkets Asda, Morrisons and Aldi. The management decided that action was needed, so it planned a new range of Waitrose Essentials – offering high quality products at 'value' prices. The result was a huge recovery, with 2009 sales rising by 12% at a time when sales at posh rival Marks & Spencer Food were still falling.

Porter's five forces

Michael Porter (author and management guru) theorised that a firm's strength depends on five key aspects, shown in the diagram below.

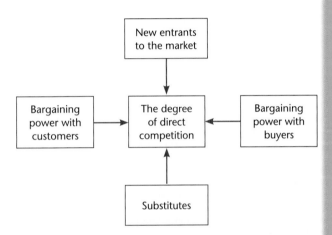

Porter's five forces can be a useful tool for analysing a firm's strength in the market and potential threats to those strengths.

A* insight

When considering a firm's corporate objectives and strategies it is useful to consider the following aspects of the organisation:

● Do the strategies help to achieve the overall objective?
● Do the objectives and strategy fit with the culture of the organisation?
● Do the strategies seem feasible given what you know about the resources of the organisation? For example, if an objective of growth is to be pursued by a strategy of taking over a rival, is the organisation's balance sheet strong enough to support this?

Test yourself (20 marks)

1　What is meant by the term 'corporate objective'? (2)
2　Why is 'to grow' not a SMART objective? (3)
3　Explain why diversification can be risky. (4)
4　Explain how diversification aims to spread risk. (4)
5　What is meant by the term 'corporate strategy'? (2)
6　State each of Porter's five forces. (5)

Unit 2 Corporate aims, mission and culture

What?

Aim – a general statement of intended direction, from which more specific goals (objectives) can be set. An example of an aim might be 'to become as big as we can be'.

Mission – an almost religious zeal to achieve something extraordinary. In the early years of Innocent Drinks, staff felt fantastic about their part in a small business that was converting people from drinking fizzy, chemical drinks to drinking 100% fruit smoothies. They felt that they were changing the world for the better, which is the effective definition of a mission.

Many managements envy the (few) businesses whose staff share a real sense of mission. To capture the same sense of inspiration, they may involve staff in devising a mission statement. This sets out the aims of the organisation but written in such a way as to inspire and enthuse stakeholders. A well-known example is: 'To refresh the world' (Coca-Cola).

Culture – the culture of an organisation is the accepted behaviours, attitudes and ideals embedded within that organisation and adopted by the workforce.

Why?

Aims

Exist to provide direction for the organisation. It forms the basis for setting the objectives.

Mission

A mission statement exists to inspire existing and potential stakeholders to take a positive view of the organisation. It may also act as a public relations tool.

Culture

Culture is something that exists regardless of whether or not it is intended to exist. It has no reason for existence – it is just there. The reasons why it is important however are numerous. It affects the behaviour and attitudes of staff and therefore can affect firms in the following ways:
- motivation
- productivity
- attitude to quality
- attitude to wastage
- absenteeism
- ethical standards.

Application

In the years that led up to the 2008 Credit Crunch, there were lots of clues about the culture (attitudes and behaviours) among investment bank staff. Courts in London and New York had revealed an extreme macho culture in which female staff were treated as second-class citizens, and drug-taking was widespread. In a series of court cases, women gained big compensation payouts in unfair dismissal cases (sacked for standing up for themselves). It was clear in 2006 and 2007 that things had got out of hand. Yet the senior directors of the banks stood back and let reckless staff do reckless things, while profits flowed in. The directors should have reacted to the amoral culture among staff by demanding wholesale changes. Instead, they blundered on until crisis hit.

Which?

The mission model

The mission model sets out in detail the value of a clear mission. Its purpose is to give a basis for four key elements within an organisation (purpose, values, strategy and standards and behaviours) to develop in the same direction.

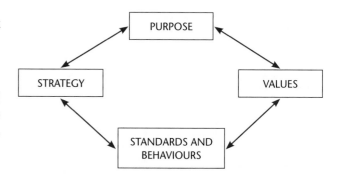

The Mission Model (Campbell, *et al*, 1990)

PURPOSE: This refers to the reason for the business to exist.

VALUES: Beliefs held by the organisation and the people it employs.

STANDARDS: The expected level of performance and quality.

STRATEGY: A medium to long-term plan for meeting objectives.

Campbell's theory suggests that the mission statement is the key to linking these four factors. Critics believe that writing a mission statement on paper achieves little; a mission statement is not the same as a real mission.

Building culture

Culture is the way that things are done and people act in an organisation. It includes the accepted and expected behaviours and attitudes in the workplace. It takes time to develop and can be affected by:

- **The attitude and behaviour of management** – This will be particularly important in small organisations where the owner/manager will tend to have a lot of contact time with employees.
- **The aims and objectives of the organisation** – An aim of profit maximisation may result in a very different organisational culture than an aim of growth or innovation.
- **The attitude of management to risk** – If management is risk averse, this will develop a culture of caution and mistake avoidance.

	Causes	Effects
An entrepreneurial culture	• The marketplace may mean there are huge new opportunities emerging, e.g. the early days of the mobile phone market. • Internal promotions given to bold decision-makers, not on seniority.	• Bright young staff want to join a business where they may have scope for taking bold new initiatives. • More initiatives mean more mistakes, but hopefully successes will outweigh failures.
A selfish, personal culture	• Payment systems with a high bonus element will make people follow the money. • If there is a hire-and-fire approach to staffing, people will protect themselves to try to keep their jobs.	• Decisions will be focused on the short-term, even if they may have awful potential consequences later. • Without teamwork and a team spirit there is no potential for bright ideas benefiting from discussion.
A highly ethical culture	• The business owners may have strong religious or moral commitments. • The ownership structure may not be profit-focused, e.g. a worker cooperative such as John Lewis.	• Business growth might be held back by refusing profit-focused shortcuts such as discussing prices with rivals (which is illegal, but quite common). • Yet John Lewis has shown that high standards can cement customer loyalty.

Exam insight

In most successful businesses aims, mission and culture fit together to provide a sound foundation for the whole organisation. If the staff believe in the company, that not only helps their motivation, but also spreads by word of mouth to potential employees. Bright young people are keen to find work at a company that seems decent and seems to be going places.

When reading a case study it is useful to consider whether the aims, mission and culture really fit together. In particular, ask yourself whether managers' actions fit with their words. If they are contradictory it would be right to suspect a public relations stunt rather than something authentic.

For example, a business may claim that its aim is to 'improve the lives of all stakeholders involved in the organisation'. Yet its workplace culture may promote short-term target-hitting behaviour and reward questionable behaviour as long as profits are generated. This contradiction would clearly suggest that the publicly-stated aim is simply for PR purposes.

Themes for evaluation

Evaluation requires questioning and judgement of the business's aims, culture or mission. This could include:
- criticism of the culture for encouraging unethical behaviour
- questioning whether the organisational aim is right in the current economic/competitive environment
- questioning whether the culture, aims and mission fit together
- judgement of whether the organisational culture is driving the organisation forward or holding it back.

Test yourself (20 marks)

1 What is the difference between an aim and an objective? (3)
2 What is the difference between an aim and a mission statement? (3)
3 Why is culture important in an organisation? (4)
4 Give two factors that can affect organisational culture. (2)
5 Why is it important that aims, mission and culture fit together rather than clash with one another? (4)
6 According to the mission model, what is the purpose of mission statements? (4)

Unit 3 Functional objectives and strategy

What?

Whereas a corporate objective is a specific goal for the whole organisation, a functional objective is a goal for a particular division of the business. These divisions (functions) are usually Marketing, Finance, People and Operations. The functional objectives should contribute to meeting the firm's overall corporate objective. The table below shows how a company-wide (corporate) objective could be broken down into goals for each business function. If the senior manager in charge of any of the four slips up, the results could be corporate failure.

Corporate objective	Marketing objective	Operations objective	Personnel (HR) objective	Financial objective
1. (For M & S) For more than 50% of sales revenue to come from under-50s within two years.	Advertising and promotions to focus on a target audience of 25–40, without alienating over-50s.	Redesign the stores so there are clearly marked-out areas with clothes for younger women.	Focus recruit-ment and training on lively, friendly personalities – to attract younger customers.	No increase expected in profit for the next two years – to finance a move away from older customers.
2. (For Leeds United) To return to the Premier League within three seasons.	To build season ticket sales to 20,000 in order to boost income by 20%.	To operate the stadium safely, but at 5% lower cost in each of the next three years.	Improve staff train-ing so that 10% fewer staff are needed to run a safe stadium.	Achieve a £20 million profit over the next three years, to finance player purchases.

Why?

It is important that each department has its own objective in order to provide focus and motivation for staff and management alike. In order to achieve these objectives, managers must draw up detailed plans of what activities need to take place and when. These are known as functional strategies.

Together functional objectives and strategies give departments a target to achieve and a plan for how to achieve it. And each department can have confidence that its plans dovetail with those of the other functions.

Which?

1 Marketing objectives

Marketing objectives tend to focus on achieving one of the following:
- increasing brand awareness
- increasing brand loyalty (and therefore, potentially, prices)
- increasing sales.

An example of a marketing objective for a shoe shop might be:

'To increase the percentage of repeat purchase customers from 5% to 20% within two years.'

Having identified the marketing objective, managers can use the marketing model as a way to decide on the right marketing strategy. In other words they will go through a careful decision-making process that involves:
- setting objectives
- gathering research data
- forming hypotheses (alternative strategies)
- testing them
- implementing the best (and reviewing performance).

In the case of a strategy to increase repeat purchases at a shoe shop, options include:
- developing a loyalty card scheme
- developing a detailed customer database in order to improve communication with existing customers
- running evening fashion shows for regular shoppers, showing off new stock.

Each would be expensive to introduce, so it's important to make the right strategic decision in the first place.

2 Financial objectives

May include:

- increasing profit margins from 8% to 10%
- increasing cash budgets available to fast-growing product lines
- improving cash flow management in order to cut interest payments.

Achieving the objective of improved profit margins would be difficult if the marketing department was – at the same time – pursuing the goal of boosting market share. The functional objectives must be coordinated.

3 Operational objectives

May include:

- increasing capacity
- reducing variable cost per unit
- improving quality.

Strategies for increasing capacity could include:

- outsourcing production of resource-intensive products
- improving productivity
- purchasing better machinery
- improving training
- improving motivation
- making more efficient use of space
- moving to a larger location.

In a business such as BMW, the power and influence of the engineering teams would ensure that the operations function would always get the resources needed to build fantastic cars. In a small glassware factory, the finance function may continually be rejecting requests for newer factory equipment. The ability to meet operational objectives may depend on the internal power and influence of each function.

4 HR objectives

- To ensure that all staff have at least five days of training in the coming financial year.
- To ensure that at least 70% of staff have degrees within five years.

Possible strategies for ensuring at least 70% of staff have degrees include:

- supporting existing staff to do part-time degrees
- starting a graduate-recruitment programme
- advertising vacancies at universities.

How?

It is not enough in business to write objectives and devise strategies. This approach can only work if sufficient resources are available. The marketing function requires an adequate marketing budget. For example, launching a brand new chocolate bar into the UK market is said to cost around £10 million. Exactly the same is true of the other functions. In operations management, spending might need to be huge, e.g. on a new, robotic production line.

Exam insight

In order to gain vital application marks it is important to answer the question in the context of the business. Some considerations you may make include:

- What are the overall aims and objectives of the business in question?
- Are the functional objectives and strategies a logical route to achieving the corporate plans?
- Are the personnel and financial resources in place?
- Has the business thought hard enough about external factors that may disrupt the achievement of the functional objectives?

Key terms

Functional objective – the goal of each division of the business: marketing, finance, people and operations.
Functional strategy – the detailed thinking and planning involved in making the functional goals achievable.

Themes for evaluation

In order to evaluate your answer you must make a judgement. Possible lines of evaluation include:

- Considering the likelihood that the objectives will be met.
- Making a judgement on how well the departments are coordinated with one another. For example, if the marketing department is launching a huge sales promotion, is the operations department prepared for the potential surge in demand? If the communication appears to be poor, whose fault is it and what could be done in the future in order to improve things?
- Is the business culture helping the firm to achieve its objectives? Or is it an obstruction?

Test yourself (20 marks)

1 What is the purpose of a functional objective? (2)
2 How are functional objectives set? (3)
3 Give two examples of marketing objectives. (2)
4 Give two examples of an operations management objective. (2)
5 Outline three constraints to a firm meeting its marketing objective to 'increase sales volumes by 10% this financial year'. (6)
6 Why is it important that the different functions communicate with one another regarding their objectives? (5)

 **Unit 4** **Responsibilities to stakeholders and society**

What?

A stakeholder is an individual or group which has an interest in the activities, successes or mistakes made by a business. It may be an individual or group which affects the business or one that is affected by the activities of the business. A bank or pressure group affects the business whereas the local community is affected by the business's actions.

Who?

```
          ┌────────────┐
          │ Employees  │
┌──────────┐ └────────────┘ ┌──────────┐
│Consumers │        │       │ Managers │
└──────────┘        │       └──────────┘
          ┌────────────┐
          │Stakeholders│
          └────────────┘
┌──────────┐   │    │   ┌──────────┐
│Shareholders│  │    │  │ Suppliers│
└──────────┘ ┌────────────┐ └──────────┘
          │   Local    │
          │ Community  │
          └────────────┘
```

Why?

Firms can be said to have a responsibility to all parties that affect or are affected by the business. Some responsibilities are legal ones (e.g. a plc's responsibility to its shareholders) whereas others are moral (a business's responsibility to the local community). Legal responsibilities must be adhered to whereas moral responsibilities are a choice.

Which?

The shareholder concept

Some believe that an organisation's primary responsibility is to its shareholders. It is they who own the business and employ the managers to run the firm. Therefore managers should act in shareholders' best interests, even if other stakeholders are made less well-off as a result.

The shareholder concept holds that:
- the objectives of shareholders should be placed over and above the objectives of other stakeholders

- in effect, therefore, profit (and – consequently – dividend payments to shareholders) maximisation should be the governing objective of the business. Company directors, who shy away from referring to profit maximisation, like to use the phrase 'maximising **shareholder value**'.

Application

In the period leading up to 2006 Cadbury boasted to the City of London that its primary objective was to maximise shareholder value, i.e. profit. At the same time the company's consumer website spoke of the company's commitment to all its stakeholders. A sign of the true focus on profit came when a cost-cutting drive resulted in salmonella food poisoning. Cadbury tried to ignore the problem until forced to withdraw more than one million chocolate bars from the UK market. Profit maximisation is always an objective that can backfire. In this case it certainly did.

The stakeholder concept

In contrast, those who believe in the stakeholder concept would argue that the objectives of all stakeholders should try to be met, rather than merely the objectives of shareholders.

This can benefit an organisation as it:
- is likely to result in a more motivated workforce (as their objectives would also be taken into account when decisions are made)
- is likely to improve the public image of the organisation. This could result in an increase in brand loyalty and, in turn, an increase in sales
- treating suppliers well may result in a better relationship; this may be very valuable when new products are being developed.

Problems

In an ideal world perhaps all firms would take a stakeholding approach. In reality this is unrealistic because:
- Different stakeholders often have very different objectives. It can be impossible to satisfy all stakeholders. For example, pollution risks at a factory may infuriate pressure groups, yet the staff themselves want to keep their jobs (despite the exposure to pollutants).
- Public limited companies (plcs) are owned by many shareholders, all of whom want share prices and dividends to rise, but few of whom feel any

personal responsibility for the company's actions. Therefore the pressure on the Board of Directors is to deliver financial success rather than a balance between profits and ethics. A stakeholder approach is much easier to achieve in a family-run business, where the family can make decisions on moral grounds – and can take a long-term view of the need to build the company's image.

Corporate Social Responsibility (CSR)

CSR refers to the extent to which firms accept their responsibilities to all stakeholder groups above the legal minimums.

As standards of living have risen in the UK, so have people's expectations of business. It used to be enough to provide a good quality product or service but in recent times consumers have come to want, and in many cases expect, more than this. Examples of possible expectations include:

- good treatment of staff in terms of pay, conditions and benefits
- keeping carbon emissions to a minimum
- ensuring that no supplier uses child labour or pays starvation wages
- donating a proportion of their profits to worthy charities.

In fact, most modern firms employ CSR professionals. They will advise on the company's website and on the appointment of a public relations agency. But so what? That is to do with publicity, not policy. The real test of a company's CSR policy comes with actions, not words. In 2009 Cadbury switched all its cocoa supplies to Fairtrade sources in Ghana. This was probably on the rebound from its salmonella humiliation in 2006/07. Even so, it may improve the lives of thousands of farmers and their families in central Africa.

Exam insight

In the exam, think hard about the circumstances of the business in question. Its willingness and ability to adopt social responsibilities will depend on various factors:

- The market circumstances. The firm may be in a ferociously competitive market where profit margins are low. In this case, a stakeholder view may be too costly, e.g. volunteering to start a pension scheme for staff.
- The culture of the organisation.
- The firm's position in the market. A business which is the lowest cost operator may not need to act in a socially responsible way as much as a firm which has a position of high quality and high customer expectations.

Key Terms

Corporate social responsibility – the extent to which firms accept their responsibilities to all stakeholder groups.
Shareholder concept – that directors' primary duty is to the shareholders – the owners of the business.
Shareholder value – maximising company profit in order to boost dividend payments and boost the share price.
Stakeholder concept – that directors should treat equally the interests of all the firm's stakeholders.

Themes for evaluation

There are two key avenues for evaluation:
1 To what extent is it necessary for this particular firm to act on behalf of stakeholders other than shareholders?
2 To what extent is it possible for the firm in question to satisfy all stakeholder groups? Do the groups have conflicting interests/objectives? If so, is there a way to keep everyone happy? How?
In asking and answering these questions, make sure you distinguish between what the company says and what it does. Some clichés deserve to be recycled: 'actions speak louder than words'.

Test yourself (20 marks)

1 Explain the difference between the stakeholder approach and the shareholder approach. (4)
2 What are the benefits of pursuing a stakeholding approach? (4)
3 State three benefits of being socially responsible. (3)
4 Why may it be difficult/impossible for a firm to satisfy all stakeholder groups? (4)
5 Why are firms becomingly increasing concerned about their social responsibility? (5)

Responsibilities to stakeholders and society

2 Advanced accounting and finance

 Unit 5 Financial objectives and constraints

What?

A financial objective states what a business aims to achieve in financial terms over a period of time. Examples of financial objectives might include:

1. Increase net profit margins from 9% to 12% within three years (which would increase the company's profit by one third, making shareholders very happy).
2. Reduce gearing (debt) levels from 60% of capital employed to 40% within the next year. This would give the business better protection from a bad trading period or a sharp economic recession.
3. Increase supplier credit periods from 60 to 90 days over the next six months. This would give a significant boost to the firm's cash position, though at the cost of the suppliers.

A constraint is something that may prevent a firm from achieving its objectives. Constraints can be internal (caused within the business) or external (caused from outside the business). The table below shows the constraints that might limit the above financial objectives.

Financial objective	Possible internal constraints	Possible external constraints
1. Increase net profit margins from 9% to 12% within three years.	• Staff resistance to cost cuts. • De-motivated staff may halt productivity gains.	• A new competitor may make price rises impossible. • Product drifts out of fashion.
2. Reduce gearing (debt) levels from 60% of capital employed to 40% within the next year.	• An exciting new product needs big investment. • Ageing equipment needs replacing.	• Economic slump means more cash needed, not less. • Weak stock market makes it hard to raise share capital.
3. Increase supplier credit periods from 60 to 90 days over the next six months.	• Buying department warn of problems getting supplies. • PR staff may worry about negative media comment.	• Unless rivals do the same, top suppliers may refuse to trade. • High interest rates make it hard for suppliers to survive.

Who?

In large businesses the financial objectives will usually be set by the CFO (chief financial officer) or the finance director, whereas in smaller organisations these decisions may be made by the MD (managing director). The impact of a new financial objective on the whole business, however, means that it would normally be discussed among the senior directors. The marketing and HR directors will be especially keen to limit the impact of new financial targets on their own departments.

How?

Before setting financial objectives, the company's overall aims and objectives should be considered. As the ability of a firm to meet objectives depends on internal and external business constraints, these must also be examined before the financial objective is decided upon. Internal constraints include all factors from within the business that may prevent objectives being met. This could include the quantity and quality of the factors of production available.

The business functions

There is another important way to analyse the internal constraints on financial objectives. Each individual function must be coordinated with the other three. In other words financial management can only work effectively in conjunction with marketing, people and operations. To sum up the key issues for revision:

- Financial considerations constrain the activities of the other three business functions.
- The other functions can constrain financial objectives.
- The balance between these two pressures is a function of:
  - the internal politics of the organisation
  - external pressures, including the views of major shareholders and the economic situation.

	Constraints upon Finance	Constraints from Finance
Marketing	• The effects of marketing are hard to measure (e.g. image-building and branding) so spending needs to be sustained over a long period.	• In hard times, Finance may cut the marketing budget in the middle of a financial year (wrecking the marketing plan).
People	• If HR insists on recruiting finance staff with overly-cautious attitudes, the Finance function may lack innovation and entrepreneurship.	• If cost-cutting is needed, Finance may start with cutbacks in the HR department – especially if HR has no strategic role in the business.
Operations	• Most of the spending in Operations is critical for the business, e.g. replacing lorries when they get too old – so Finance *has* to find the cash.	• Finance might insist on a 10% cost-cutting programme that forces Operations to find new, lower-cost (and lower quality?) suppliers.

External constraints include all factors from the external environment that may affect a firm's ability to meet objectives. If, for example, house prices are plummeting, it may be hugely difficult for a construction firm to increase sales. Therefore a financial objective may be to reduce costs, rather than increase profit.

Key terms

External constraint – a factor outside the firm's control that can limit its ability to meet its objectives.
Internal constraint – a factor within the business that can limit its ability to meet its objectives.

Application

Apple's development and launch of the iPhone was a business classic. Apple's boss, Steve Jobs, decided on the strategic potential of an Apple phone, then ensured that the development and – later – marketing teams had all the resources they needed. This was expensive, with development costs estimated to be more than $500 million. In this case, the financial objective was to support the marketing initiative. In the best-run companies, this will always be the way. The job of the finance department is to oil the wheels, not to decide which direction the car should take.

Exam insight

In a well-run business, financial objectives should never be imposed without discussion between the business functions. If the marketing department has a fantastic new product coming up, it would be crazy to cramp its potential because Finance has decided on a cost-cutting programme. Therefore it is wise to look for signs of how an objective came about. Has it been a matter of careful discussion? Or has it been imposed?

Themes for evaluation

In poorly-run businesses, the power of the Finance department varies. In good times, Finance simply has to come up with the money required to meet the ambitious demands of Operations and Marketing. Then, when times get tough, Finance takes charge, imposing cutbacks and demanding evidence of the need for every pound of spending. In other businesses, Finance is always in charge, restricting other departments from spending. In the best businesses, Finance will always have a say, but not <u>the</u> say. McDonald's became a giant through brilliant operations and marketing; so did Coca-Cola, L'Oréal and Apple. The most important constraint on Finance should be the business culture – entrepreneurial, customer-focused and outgoing.

Test yourself (15 marks)

1 Give two examples of financial objectives for the latest children's must have for Christmas. (2)
2 Explain one possible internal constraint and one possible external constraint to each of your financial objectives above. (8)
3 Explain one strategy the firm could employ to minimise the effect of the above constraints. (5)

Financial objectives and constraints

Unit 6 Income statements

What?

An income statement is a financial document showing the revenue, expenses, and ultimately profit of a business over a period of time (usually one year).

Why?

The purpose of an income statement is to provide stakeholder groups with a detailed breakdown of the income, expenses, and profit made by a firm over a given trading period.

It is useful to get a detailed breakdown as it may be possible to identify ways to increase the profit. For example, if rising administrative expenses have resulted in a reduction in profit from one year to the next, the management may decide that it is time to cut back in this area of the business.

Revenue

Revenue is the total value of the sales of a business over a period of time. It is not the same as cash inflow as it includes both cash sales and credit sales. It can be calculated by the formula Price × Quantity.

$$\text{Revenue} = \text{Price} \times \text{Quantity}$$

Cost of sales/cost of goods sold

This is the total cost of all the goods used in the business over a given trading period. An accountant would tell you that the correct formula is:

$$\text{Cost of goods sold} =$$
$$\text{Opening stock} + \text{Purchases} - \text{Closing stock}$$

However, on published plc income statements this calculation has already been made. Therefore it is more important to know that cost of goods amounts to all the variable and fixed operating costs that can be linked to the goods that generated the revenue. For a clothes shop, this would be the cost of purchasing all the garments that have been sold, plus the costs of running the shop over that period of time (the electricity, the salaries and so on).

The lower the cost of goods sold, the higher the gross profit will be. Cost of goods sold can be minimised by:

- **Minimising stock wastage** – This could be done by more frequent ordering of smaller quantities, better stock control, or leaner production processes.
- **Negotiating better prices with suppliers** – This could be achieved by agreeing to purchase a larger number of the same product from suppliers, agreeing to purchase a wider range of products from the same supplier, or by forming good, trusted relationships with key suppliers.
- **Shopping around to find the cheapest supplier.**

Gross profit

Gross profit is calculated by deducting the cost of goods sold from the revenue. It shows how much money has been generated on trading activity alone. However, it does not take into account overheads/expenses for the head office, such as salaries and rent.

$$\text{Gross profit} = \text{Revenue} - \text{Cost of goods sold}$$

Gross profit can be improved by:
- increasing revenue
- reducing cost of goods sold.

Expenses

Expenses are the overhead costs of running a business. The higher the expenses the lower the net profit. Therefore it is vital that management control expenses in order to maximise profits. Examples of expenses include:
- rent
- electricity
- water
- salaries
- stationery
- telephone bill.

Net profit

Net profit is calculated by deducting the total expenses from gross profit. This is a truer measure of the profit made by a firm as it takes all costs into account.

$$\text{Net profit} = \text{Gross profit} - \text{Expenses}$$

Sample income statement

Income statement for ABC Ltd

	£000s
Revenue	1300
Cost of goods sold	400
Gross profit	900
Expenses	
Salaries	300
Rent	120
Electricity	60
Depreciation	30
Water	10
Total expenses	520
Net profit	380

When?

All plcs must publish detailed accounts on a yearly basis. Private limited companies must also produce annual accounts that will be made available for anyone to look up. Only businesses with unlimited liability can avoid the need to publish their accounts. In addition, plcs will often publish quarterly (three monthly) information in order to provide stakeholders with more frequent, up-to-date information about the company's financial performance.

Application

It is important to consider the nature of the business in question when analysing its income statement. Some businesses, by nature, will have high cost of sales (e.g. an antiques shop) whereas other firms will naturally have relatively high expenses (e.g. businesses with labour intensive production methods). Therefore it is useful to look at the previous year's gross and net profit in order to make meaningful comparisons.

Key terms

Income statement – a financial document showing the revenue, expenses and profit of a business over a period of time.
Revenue – the value of the total sales of a business over a given trading period.
Cost of goods sold – the total cost of all the goods used in the business over a given trading period. Formula for cost of sales = Opening stock + Purchases – Closing stock
Expenses – the overhead costs of running a business. E.g. water, rent, electricity
Gross profit – the total profit from trading activity alone, before expenses have been deducted. Formula for gross profit = Revenue – Cost of goods sold.
Net profit – the profit that a business has made over a given trading period. Formula for net profit = Gross profit – Expenses

A* Insight

When analysing an income statement, a key question is 'What is the profit quality?' High quality profit comes from regular trading that can be expected to continue into the future. Low quality profit is a one-off, e.g. from selling the company's HQ building at a big profit. The test of a business such as Tesco is in the High Street, not in property dealings.

Themes for evaluation

In order to evaluate a firm's financial performance it is useful to look at more than merely the income statement. To get a true picture of the firm's performance it is important to also analyse the balance sheet and conduct ratio analysis. However, some important conclusions can be drawn from the income statement alone:

- By comparing revenue from two or more consecutive trading periods, a trend might be identified. It is important not just to consider the direction in which revenue is moving (i.e. is it growing or in decline?) but also to consider the extent of the growth. In order to do this the percentage change in sales could be calculated and analysed. Comparing revenues also allows one to consider the growth in the business and perhaps compare that with growth in the market as a whole. Marks & Spencer might boast to shareholders that their food sales are 6% up on a year ago. But if food sales generally are 8% up, there is nothing to boast about.
- Movement in the net profit from one year to the next tells the reader whether the firm is making more or less profit and the extent of this change. As a key business objective is often to increase profit, this may be an important way to evaluate the overall business performance.
- It is also important to judge the quality of profit and the potential reasons for increases in costs. High profit quality occurs from sources which are likely to continue into the future – e.g. trading activity, sales of new products in particular. Low-profit quality comes from one-off activities – e.g. selling off a fixed asset. In order to evaluate it is important to consider how high or low the quality of net profit is.
- When looking at the costs it is important to consider the possible reasons and effect of the increase in costs. If, for example, a 20% increase in cost of sales has occurred in the trading period but this has resulted in a 20% increase in revenue, all things being equal, profit will have risen so it would be silly to suggest that the rise in cost of sales is in any way problematic. Equally a rapid increase in advertising spending in a period in which revenue increased significantly should also not be judged negatively.

Test yourself (20 marks)

1 Who are the users of an income statement? (3)
2 What is the purpose of an income statement? (3)
3 How can gross profit be calculated? (2)
4 How can net profit be calculated? (2)
5 How can gross profit be improved? (2)
6 How can net profit be improved? (4)
7 Give two examples of situations where a rise in costs may be deemed acceptable. (4)

Unit 7 Balance sheets

What?

A balance sheet is a document listing all a firm's assets and liabilities at a point in time. That point is usually the last day of a firm's financial year. In effect, it shows what the business is worth, as measured by what it owns (assets) and what it owes (liabilities). After the liabilities are taken away from the assets, anything left belongs to the shareholders (who own the company).

The total value of a firm's assets minus the value of its external liabilities is equal to the capital invested and reinvested by shareholders (total equity). Therefore this formula always applies:

Total assets – External liabilities = Total equity

Why?

The balance sheet gives potential investors and other stakeholder groups an insight into the financial position of the organisation. This is important because firms can only trade with each other if they are confident they will be paid. Checking a customer's balance sheet is an essential starting point. If a manufacturer sees that a retail chain's balance sheet looks weak, it will refuse to sell on credit, and may not be willing to trade at all.

When?

Unlike income statements, balance sheets do not show the business's performance over a period of time (usually one year) but are a snapshot of what the business owns (assets) and owes (liabilities) at a point in time. The fact that the balance sheet is a snapshot can be a serious weakness. It opens up the possibility of window dressing, i.e. acting before the balance sheet date in a way that hides an underlying problem from outsiders. For example, if a firm's liquidity position was weak and getting worse, selling a piece of property would bring in cash to mask the problem. Outsiders will struggle to recognise that the worsening liquidity position may force the firm into ever-more panicky actions.

Which?

Assets

● **Fixed assets**
First on a balance sheet are **non-current (fixed)**

assets (items which are intended to be used for a relatively long period of time). For example, vehicles, premises or equipment. These are put on a balance sheet at their depreciated valuation. In other words a three year old company car bought for £30,000 will be valued at around £12,000, not the purchase price.

● **Current assets**
Current assets include inventory (stock), trade receivables (debtors) and cash. These are assets which are relatively liquid, meaning they can be quickly and easily turned into cash. These should be stated in order with the least liquid first and the most liquid last. As stock must be sold in order to become cash it comes first, followed by debtors and then cash.

● **Current liabilities**
Current liabilities are debts which should be paid within a one year period. These include trade creditors, bank overdraft and unpaid bills such as tax or electricity owing.

● **Long-term liabilities**
These are debts which do not need to be paid in the next year. They could include bank loans and debentures.

● **Net current assets** (also known as working capital)
This is calculated by the formula:

Net current assets = Current assets – Current liabilities

It shows how much of a firm's short-term assets (current assets) the business will have left after paying off their short-term debts (current liabilities). If the figure is negative, the implication is that the business has more short-term debts than assets. This suggests a poor liquidity position.

A* Insight

The weakness of the exam system is that it measures knowledge on just one day. So the student who has been under-performing all year might – a day or two before – revise enough to look good on the day. Shortly afterwards they have forgotten what they memorised – they are back to normal. Balance sheets can be the same. They are only a snapshot in time. Therefore firms can 'window-dress' their balance sheets to make their accounts look good. On their 'exam day' (the last day of the financial year) the balance sheet may look better than on the other 364 days of the year.

Structure of a modern balance sheet

(conforming to 2005 International Financial Reporting standards):
Non-current (fixed) assets
+
Current assets
=
Total assets

Total assets
−
Current + Non-current (long-term) liabilities
=
Net assets

Net assets
=
Total equity
(Share capital + Reserves)

Sample balance sheet

Balance sheet for Alan Burns plc
for 31st December 20XX

	£	£
NON-CURRENT ASSETS		
Premises	300,000	
Vehicles	50,000	350,000
CURRENT ASSETS		
Inventory (stock)	20,000	
Trade receivables (debtors)	18,000	
Cash	5,000	43,000
CURRENT LIABILITIES		
Creditors	(20,000)	
NON-CURRENT (LONG-TERM) LIABILITIES		
Long-term loans	(65,000)	(85,000)
NET ASSETS:	308,000	308,000
Share capital	230,000	
Reserves	78,000	
TOTAL EQUITY	308,000	308,000

Application

One year's balance sheet for an individual firm would be hard to interpret. Ideally you would also have last year's data plus the figures for a similar-sized competitor. To analyse the data, the usual tool is accounting ratios (see Unit 8).

Key terms

Current asset – an asset that can be quickly and easily turned into cash e.g. receivables, inventory and cash.
Current liability – a debt that must be paid within one year e.g. trade repayables
Non-current asset – an asset to be used and re-used over several years e.g. buildings and machinery
Non-current liability – a debt that does not have to be paid in the sort term e.g. bank loans and debentures

Themes for evaluation

There are many questions that balance sheets can help to answer. For example:
● Is the business in a position to fund a takeover bid for a rival?
● Is it in a healthy enough financial position for an investor to risk buying the shares?
● Is it a well-run business? If it claims to operate a JIT system, are its stock levels lower than its rivals? If not, why not?

However, before drawing too many conclusions from the balance sheet, it would be wise to consider:

What other information is known? The trend in a firm's market share may be far more important than the trend in its (past) profits. It is important to look at the balance sheet, but also consider other numerical data plus the information provided in text/case study material.

What are the limitations of using balance sheets to analyse financial health? Why may they sometimes not show an organisation in its true light?

How strong is the balance sheet? The stronger the balance sheet the more able a firm may be to take risks. If it is financially healthy it may be able to bear the risk of releasing a potentially huge product with only a 60% chance of succeeding in the market. However, if the financial position is worrying the firm may be unable to take such a risk, as failure may prove disastrous.

Is working capital positive or negative? Does the business have more short-term assets than liabilities? This is hugely important, especially when the competitive/economic environment is unfavourable.

Test yourself (15 marks)

1 State two users of a balance sheet. (2)
2 State two non-current assets and two current assets. (4)
3 Explain what is meant by working capital. (3)
4 State how working capital is calculated. (2)
5 Explain why capital employed is always equal to assets employed. (4)

Unit 8 Accounting ratios

What?

Balance sheets and profit and loss accounts provide information to stakeholders about the financial performance of a business over a period of time. However, knowing a business has made a profit of £50m means little without knowing the size of the business. Ratios enable comparisons to be made between firms of different sizes.

Which?

Profitability

Profitability ratios measure the profit in relation to the sales revenue, or in relation to the capital employed.

Gross profit margin

$$\text{Gross profit margin} = \frac{\text{Gross profit}}{\text{Revenue}} \times 100$$

Gross profit is annual sales revenue *minus* cost of sales (such as purchases). Profit margin measures gross profit as a percentage of sales. It shows how efficient a firm is at turning sales into gross profit, and therefore how well it controls the cost of its sales.

Ways to improve gross profit margin:
- reduce stock wastage
- negotiate with suppliers in order to reduce cost of stock
- find a cheaper supplier to reduce cost of stock
- increase price.

Net (operating) profit margin

$$\text{Net (operating) profit margin} = \frac{\text{Net profit}}{\text{Revenue}} \times 100$$

Net profit is the profit after deduction of all operating costs. On published accounts, look for the figure for operating profit. Net profit margin measures net profit as a percentage of sales revenue. It shows how efficiently a firm turns sales into net profit, and therefore how well it controls all its operating costs (cost of sales + expenses).

Ways to improve net profit margin:
- cut expenses while maintaining sales
- increase sales while keeping expenses the same
- cut cost of sales
- increase price.

Return on capital employed

$$\text{Return on capital employed} = \frac{\text{Operating profit}}{\text{Capital employed}} \times 100$$

This ratio (sometimes known as the primary efficiency ratio) measures how much profit has been made from the funds invested in the business. Therefore it shows how efficient the firm is at turning funds or capital into profit.

Interpretation

The higher the figure the more efficiently the firm turns its capital into profit. Therefore the higher the figure the better.

It can be compared with the current interest rate. After all it is the return on investment (as is the bank rate). However, the return on capital should be substantially higher than the bank rate as it is much riskier to invest money in a business than to put that money in the bank.

Ways to improve return on capital employed:
- increase net profit
- reduce capital employed while maintaining profit level.

Financial efficiency ratios

These ratios measure how effectively business is using its working capital and total capital.

Stock/inventory turnover

$$\text{Stock/inventory turnover} = \frac{\text{Cost of goods sold}}{\text{Inventory (Stock)}}$$

Expressed as number of times per year

The stock turnover shows how often a year a firm turns over (i.e. sells) its inventory. If the answer is three, this means the inventory is sold three times each year.

Interpretation

- In general the higher the figure the better, as it shows that inventory is being sold more quickly.
- However, stock turnover figures cannot be compared across industries as figures differ hugely from industry to industry. For example, fresh fish should be turned over every couple of days (maybe 200 times a year) whereas antiques may only be turned over a few times a year (three or four times a year).

- What is important when interpreting the figure is that it fits with the nature of the product. For example, if something perishable is being sold it is hugely important that the stock turnover is high.

Debtor days

$$\text{Debtor days} = \frac{\text{Debtors/trade receivables}}{\text{Annual revenue}}$$

Expressed as number of days

This shows how long, on average, a firm takes to collect debts from customers. The longer it takes, the less efficient the firm is at collecting its debts.

Improving the ratio:
To improve the ratio debts must be collected more efficiently. Ways of doing this include:
- chasing customers for payment
- giving early/cash payment discounts
- fining late payments
- improving communication with customers.

Creditor days

$$\text{Creditor days} = \frac{\text{Payables/Creditors}}{\text{Cost of sales}} \times 100$$

This measures how long it takes the firm to pay its suppliers.

Interpretation

- It should be around 30–90 days depending on the firms negotiated credit terms.
- It should not be too short as this suggests the firm is paying too early which may harm its cash flow position.
- It should not be too long as this may damage the firm's relationship with suppliers.
- It can be shortened by paying debts more quickly.

Asset turnover ratio

$$\text{Asset turnover} = \frac{\text{Annual sales revenue}}{\text{Assets employed}} \times 100$$

Asset turnover measures how much money a firm generates from sales as a proportion of the assets it owns.

Interpretation

The higher the figure the more efficiently the firm generates revenue from its asset base.

How high this should be depends on the profit margins. If a firm has low asset turnover (i.e. produces little sales revenue from its assets) this can be compensated for if its profit margins are very high.

Improving asset turnover:
There are two key ways to improve asset turnover:
- increase sales using the same asset base
- maintain sales whilst selling off underutilised assets.

Liquidity ratios

These ratios measure the short-term financial health of the business.

Current ratio/liquidity ratio

$$\text{Current ratio} = \frac{\text{Current assets}}{\text{Current liabilities}}$$

This is expressed as an actual ratio. For example 1:1. This means that for each £1 of current assets the firm has £1 of current liabilities. Whereas 2:1 would mean the firm has £2 of current assets for every £1 of current liabilities.

Interpreting the ratio

Accountants suggest that a ratio of 1.5:1 is ideal as any higher suggests assets are being underutilised and any lower runs a risk that the business will be unable to pay its short-term debts.

Acid test ratio

Some assets are more liquid (i.e. easier to turn into cash) than others. The least liquid of the current assets is stock as it must be sold in order to be turned into cash. Therefore the acid-test still looks at the ratio between current assets and current liabilities but deducts stock from the current assets.

$$\text{Acid test ratio} = \frac{\text{Current asset} - \text{Stock}}{\text{Current liabilities}}$$

This is also expressed as a ratio. E.g. 2.5:1

Interpreting the ratio

When stock is deducted from current assets the current assets will be comparatively smaller compared to the current liabilities therefore accountants suggest a ratio of around 1:1 is ideal.

Gearing

Gearing measures the percentage of a firm's capital employed which comes from long-term liabilities. The formula is as follows:

$$\text{Gearing} = \frac{\text{Non-current (long-term) liabilities}}{\text{Capital employed}} \times 100$$

Interpreting gearing level

If the gearing level is higher than 50% the firm is said to be highly geared. This means that loans represent a worryingly high proportion of capital employed. Being highly geared increases the costs of a firm as they will incur huge interest charges. Also the higher the gearing level, the higher the degree of risk. Banks may be unwilling to lend to firms with high gearing as they will be less confident that the business will be able to pay back the loan.

However, it is also important to note that very low gearing is not necessarily a positive thing. It may suggest they have been overly cautious and will be unable to benefit from the rapid growth that borrowing can facilitate.

Shareholder ratios

These ratios show what shareholders receive as a return on their investment.

Earnings per share

Earnings per share measures how much profit has been made for each share sold in the organisation. It is calculated by the formula:

$$\text{Earnings per share} = \frac{\text{Profit after tax}}{\text{Number of shares}}$$

It shows how much potential there is for the firm to pay out dividends to shareholders. However, in order to have real meaning it must be compared with previous year's results. The higher it is the higher the potential for dividends to be paid.

Dividend per share

This ratio shows the dividend that each share will receive. It is calculated by the formula:

$$\text{Dividend per share} = \frac{\text{Total dividends}}{\text{Shares issued}}$$

This figure can then be compared with the share price (dividend yield) to give it a context for comparison.

Dividend yield

$$\text{Dividend yield} = \frac{\text{Ordinary share dividend}}{\text{Market price of share}} \times 100$$

This shows the return (dividend) as a percentage of the market value of the share.

Interpretation

The higher the percentage, the higher the return on investment. Using this ratio one can compare the performance of one firm with another.

Exam insight

A classic phrase is that 'ratios don't answer questions, they only raise them'. In other words, beware of jumping to conclusions about a firm with a low acid test ratio or a high return on capital. The ideal situation is to have two or three years' worth of ratios, so that you can start to see a trend. Then you can start to think about possible causes or effects.

Themes for evaluation

Although it is useful to look at one ratio in isolation, it is often more useful to consider more than one factor at a time. For example, if the net profit margin has fallen from 10% to 9% that may at first sight seem like the business's performance has slipped but if the revenue has jumped from £12m to £16m, then overall the profit will actually have increased from £1.2m to £1.44m. It can be useful when evaluating performance to consider things which may have caused ratios to appear worse/better than they truly are.

Test yourself (20 marks)

1 Explain why ratio analysis is useful. (4)
2 Explain the term 'liquidity'. (3)
3 What is the difference between the acid test ratio and the current ratio? (3)
4 Outline two ways to improve a firm's profitability. (4)
5 Why may low gearing in a booming economic climate make investors less inclined to invest? (6)

Unit 9 Limitations of accounts

What?

Although a good deal of information is available from considering a firm's income statement, balance sheet and resulting ratios, this information can give an incomplete or even misleading view of a business's worth or success.

Why?

Focus on purely quantitative data

Although a lot can be gleaned from looking at numerical data it does not take into account other vital factors such as management quality, staff loyalty and motivation, strategic planning or commitment to ethics. For example, a drive to create a more environmentally friendly product may, in the short-term, increase costs and thus reduce short-term profit margins. In the long term, though, it may improve the reputation of the firm, increase brand loyalty and therefore sales and profitability.

Focus too strongly on profit

Profit, although important, may sometimes have to be sacrificed in the short term in order to generate further success in the long term. Using profit as a key performance measure may encourage managers/ owners to be short-termist. Furthermore, profit may be a good measure of short-term success but not of future potential.

Historical data

Business accounts reflect what has happened in the past and not what may happen in the future. The state of the economy, market and consumer trends and competitor behaviour all need to be taken into account when considering future performance.

For well-established companies during good and stable economic times there may be little difference between revenue or profit from one year to the next. However, when the global recession struck in autumn 2008 many businesses could not have relied on past data to assess (even roughly) what was likely to happen in times to follow. Suddenly credit became virtually impossible to come by, cash became the key resource and cost minimisation the key strategy.

Margin for error

In his 2009 book *Margins of Error in Accounting* Professor D.R. Myddelton makes two fundamental points:

1 That every set of accounts should be seen as 'interim'. In other words, accounts are a work in progress; because the transactions within a large business are complex and numerous, it is impossible to know exactly what profit was made within a specific period of time. We now know that the vast 'profits' claimed to have been made by banks such as HBOS and Lehman Brothers in 2007 were a complete illusion. Effectively both firms went bust in 2008.

2 That effective accounting is based on judgement. The book warns about 'spurious precision', for example the claim that a company's profit was £1,678,652 in a year. The Professor explains that much of accounting is based on estimates, not recorded, known data. Therefore he urges the readers and users of accounts to:

- 'be alert to signs of possible trouble, such as: late accounts; directors resigning; a change of auditors
- consider using three year averages for some ratios if reported profits are volatile
- look at five year or ten year trends, as well as the latest year's results
- don't expect too much'.

From *Margins of Error in Accounting*, D.R. Myddelton, Palgrave Macmillan 2009.

Problems with interpretation

Valuing of assets – It can be difficult to estimate asset values and accountants may value assets at their historical cost (i.e. the price that was paid for the asset) rather than value them at their current value.

Stock value – Stock is only worth what somebody is willing to pay for it at a point in time. Looking at the balance sheet, the reader can see how much the stock is 'worth' on paper but this does not mean that someone is willing to actually buy it at this price. That depends on the nature of the stock. For example, Christmas cards are worth virtually nothing in January.

Profit quality – Profit quality refers to how likely the profit source is to continue in the future. A one-off sale of an asset would be said to have a very low profit quality whereas sales of a new product would result in a much higher profit quality. Looking just at the profit margins, the profit quality cannot be determined. However with careful examination of the profit and loss account itself, this information will be available.

Window dressing – Means to manipulate accounts in order to show the business in the best possible light. This can mislead the users of accounts into believing the business is in a better position than it truly is.

Possible ways of improving the appearance of accounts:

- Selling off fixed assets to improve the cash position and therefore liquidity.
- Encouraging customers to order earlier so as to bring sales into the current accounting period.
- Changing the method of depreciation in order to reduce expenses and boost profit. This may help to attract investors.

The Companies Act

The Companies Act 1988 places a legal obligation on companies to provide audited accounts that give a true and fair reflection of the firm's financial position.

Key terms

Limitation – something which limits or reduces the usefulness or reliability of accounts.

Profit quality – a judgement of whether a firm's reported profit is based largely on items that will generate further profit in future years. Therefore one-off profits are low quality.

Quantitative data – data which comes in numerical form including the income statement, balance sheet and ratios.

Window dressing – taking actions that present the published accounts in a better light than would otherwise be the case. This may prevent outsiders from becoming aware of serious problems faced by the business.

A* Insight

Although every business will window-dress its accounts to an extent, the vast majority are 99% honest and open. A much more widespread problem is time, i.e. that *all* published accounts are a record of the past. If circumstances have changed dramatically since the end of the last financial year, the 'latest accounts' may be obsolete. This matters enormously for firms that depend upon one product or brand, especially if the firm operates in a short product life cycle sector.

Application

The context of the business in question needs to be considered in order to analyse the potential limitations of the business's accounts. If, for example, it states in the text that the business is currently in search of further investment then it has an incentive to overstate profit. However, if the business is stable and seeking to cut costs, it might overstate its expenses where possible in order to understate profit. This would reduce its corporation (profit) tax payments.

Themes for evaluation

This topic itself is a useful source of evaluation. Questions about ratios can be evaluated by judging the limitations of the specific company's accounts. What evidence is there that window dressing is happening? Is there evidence in the text that short-term profits are being sacrificed in order to boost long-term potential for growth, in which case dwindling profit margins may be deemed acceptable.

It is also vital to consider the information given to you in the case study in order to assess the limitations of the accounts. If the information in the case conflicts with that suggested by the quantitative data this could well be an avenue to explore.

Test yourself (20 marks)

1 Explain the following terms:
   a) spurious precision
   b) window dressing. (4)
2 Explain why profit may not always be the best indicator of a firm's performance. (4)
3 Explain three ways a firm could show its accounts in a better light. (6)
4 What does the Companies Act state? (2)
5 Explain two problems with interpreting accounts. (4)

Unit 10 Financial strategies and accounts

What?

A financial strategy is a long-term financial plan devised to support the overall business objective. Financial strategies may include: raising finance, allocating capital expenditure, cost minimisation and implementing cost and/or profit centres.

Which?

Raising finance

Firms may need to raise finance in order to:
- grow
- for specific purchases
- to cope with financial difficulties.

Finance can be raised internally or externally.
Internal sources of finance include:
- retained profit
- sale of assets
- managing working capital.

Advantages: cheaper than using external sources as no interest payments

no need to sell a part of the company

Disadvantages: limited to available finance within the business

opportunity cost.

External sources include:
- bank loan
- bank overdraft
- venture capital
- share capital.

Analysis

At A2, the key aspect to raising finance is to see it in relation to A2 factors such as the balance sheet and methods of investment appraisal. Using internal sources of finance can stretch the liquidity of a business. That might be fine in good times, but in tough years such as 2008 and 2009, cash in the bank was the thing to have. The producer of Crocs shoes spent 2006 and 2007 buying up other shoe producers. It had cash in the bank and wanted to use it. Suddenly, in the changed circumstances of 2008, it was fighting for survival – desperate to find cash from anywhere.

With external finance, the key is the balance between debt and equity, i.e. between borrowing more and raising more from ('equity') shareholders. Another business that was lucky to survive 2008 was Britain's biggest housebuilder, Barratt Homes.

It bought another housebuilder in 2007 for over £2 billion. Its bank had advised it to borrow the whole sum. Luckily it ignored the advice and raised a quarter of the sum from a shareholders' rights issue. This stopped its gearing getting quite so high, and Barratt just scraped through 2008.

Exam insight

When considering which source of finance a business should use it is vital that you choose an appropriate source for the given case, i.e. the type of finance matches the use. For example, short-term needs for finance (e.g. manage cash flow) should be met with short-term finance (e.g. overdraft).

The source must also be realistic/feasible for the firm. For example, it is not feasible for a start-up business to use retained profits as a source as they will not have any.

Or if a business is very highly geared (e.g. 65%) it is inappropriate to suggest they take out a bank loan as the bank is very unlikely to agree to this.

Allocating capital expenditure

Capital expenditure is money which is spent by firms with a view to improving long-term operations. It could be the purchase of fixed assets (e.g. machinery/factory) or financing a takeover bid.

Things to consider when allocating capital expenditure:

- Opportunity cost
The money that could be used will always hold an opportunity cost – i.e. there are other things that the money could be spent on. Therefore whether this is the best use of finance available must be considered before a decision is made.

- How much is needed
The amount of money a firm uses on capital expenditure will depend on various factors including:
  - how much money is available
  - how essential the spending is
  - the potential long-term rewards
  - the extent to which the expenditure will help the firm to meet its objectives.

Implementing profit centres

A profit centre is a part of a business which can be measured in terms of costs and revenues and therefore profit.

Take Tesco for example. It is a huge organisation so as well as knowing how the whole business has performed financially, management will also want to get a more detailed breakdown of performance. They will look at the revenue, costs and profit made by each individual store. Therefore in the case of Tesco each store is a profit centre.

Profit centres can be based on:

1 **Product** – E.g. Apple: the iPod is a profit centre as is the iPhone.
2 **Department** – Different departments in an organisation may act as profit centres.
3 **Store's branches** – E.g. Tesco.

Benefits of profit centres

- Helps firms to identify poorly performing areas of the organisation. These areas can then be helped to improve or possibly closed down if necessary.
- May act as a performance incentive to managers, if they have responsibility for their profit centre's performance.
- Helps to identify highly profitable areas of the business. They could be used as examples of best practice or managers of effective profit centres may be used to train other managers.

Problems with profit centres

- Not every cost (or revenue) can be easily attributed to specific areas of the business.
- It may be unfair to judge management by the area's results as they may depend on factors beyond their control (e.g. a flood in Birmingham may affect McDonald's in Birmingham).
- Implementation may cause competition between areas of the business leading to each unit working for its own objectives rather than the overall company objectives e.g. a branch may sacrifice long-term customer satisfaction for short term profits by selling stock which does not meet a high measure of quality.

Cost minimisation

This is a financial strategy which requires the firm to keep costs to an absolute minimum. It has two possible motivations:

1 **In order to increase competitiveness** – Reducing costs enables firms to reduce prices in order to be more competitive in the market. This is particularly likely in highly competitive markets.
2 **In order to increase profit margins** – If this is the motivation, reductions in costs will not result in a drop in price but price will remain the same thus resulting in rising profit margins.

Cost minimisation may be a key financial strategy when:

- quality of products will not be severely affected
- consumers are fundamentally driven by price
- profit margins need to be increased (possibly due to pressure from shareholders).

Concerns with cost minimisation

As Porter outlined in his theory of generic strategies, one path to business security is to be the lowest cost operator. The concern for firms who seek to cost minimise is that it is vital to be the lowest. If other firms enter the market with a lower price, this might destroy a firm which has price as its USP. The only way to make money from this strategy is with huge sales volumes as margins tend to be very low.

Themes for evaluation

The following are possible avenues for evaluation:

- How logical are the key financial strategies of the business given the current situation of the business outlined in the case?
- To what extent do the financial strategies fit with the organisation's objectives?
- How important are the financial strategies outlined? Are there any other strategies which you believe to be more important in the circumstances?
- Long-term versus short-term. Is one strategy going to be preferable in the short term and another in the long-term? If so, which, why and which is most important? NOTE: Do not always assume that the long-term is more important. In tough economic times surviving in the short-term sometimes becomes the key and therefore a strategy of cost minimisation may be necessary.

Test yourself (20 marks)

1 Why may a firm need to raise finance? (3)
2 State two internal sources of finance. (2)
3 State two possible external sources of finance. (2)
4 What must a manager consider when deciding how to allocate capital expenditure? (4)
5 Explain one disadvantage of pursuing a financial strategy of cost minimisation. (3)
6 Explain two possible reasons for a firm to pursue a strategy of cost minimisation. (6)

 **Unit 11** Investment appraisal

What?

Investment appraisal is a set of techniques used to evaluate the expected financial gains of investing in a long-term project. This is done by forecasting the likely future cash flows from the project and comparing them with the initial cost. The purpose is to help in making the decision: do we go ahead or not? Or, which one of the options do we choose?

Decisions which may require conducting an investment appraisal include:

- Should XY Ltd buy a new factory in the UK or shift production to China?
- Should XY Ltd open a second branch or not?
- Should ABC Ltd launch product A or product B?

Why?

When considering whether or not to invest in a project there are two key questions the investor will want the answer to:

1 How much money will I make?
2 When will I get the money back?

Investment appraisal seeks to answer both of these questions. It must always be remembered, though, that the appraisal will be based on estimated future cash flows. This is hard for existing businesses – and terribly hard for brand new firms that do not yet understand their market fully. Forecasting the future for a business is a bit like weather forecasting: reasonably accurate for tomorrow, less accurate for a week's time, and ever-flakier as the months or years go by.

Investment appraisal is used by every large firm and every government department. Unfortunately that does not mean that it's accurate.

Which?

Payback period

This method focuses on when the money will be returned. This is done by working out at which point the net cash flow repays in full the sum invested – i.e. when cumulative cash is zero.

Example

Year	Cash in (£s)	Cash out (£s)	Net cash	Cumulative cash
0	0	100,000	(100,000)	(100,000)
1	30,000	20,000	10,000	(90,000)
2	40,000	25,000	15,000	(75,000)
3	50,000	30,000	20,000	(55,000)
4	66,000	35,000	31,000	(24,000)
5	70,000	22,000	48,000	24,000

In the example above, the investment is recouped after the end of year 4, but before the end of year 5. At the beginning of year 5 £24,000 is still needed. At the end they have £24,000 extra so cumulative cash would be zero exactly halfway through year 5.

Payback period = 4 years and 6 months.

The formula to calculate the months is:

Number of months = Outlay outstanding / Monthly net cash in year of payback

In this case the outlay outstanding is £24,000 and the monthly net cash in year 5 is £48,000/12 = £4000, therefore:

Number of months = $\frac{\text{Outlay outstanding}}{\text{Monthly net cash in year of payback}} = \frac{£24,000}{£4,000} = 6$ months

Interpretation

- The shorter the payback period the more willing firms/individuals will be to invest.
- The shorter the payback period the lower the opportunity cost of missing out on having that money in the bank accumulating interest.
- The shorter the payback period the less time the company's money is at risk.

Average rate of return

The method calculates the average annual return (profit) of an investment as a percentage of the original sum invested. It allows comparisons to be made between two or more investment opportunities or comparisons with bank interest rates.

$$ARR = \frac{\text{Average annual return}}{\text{Initial outlay}} \times 100$$

Average annual return can be calculated by the formula:

$$\frac{\text{Total profit over lifetime of project}}{\text{Number of years}}$$

Example

Year	Net cash flow (£s)	Cumulative cash flow (£s)
0	(60,000)	(60,000)
1	10,000	(50,000)
2	20,000	(30,000)
3	35,000	5,000
4	31,000	36,000

Average annual return = £36,000/4 = £9000

Average rate of return = £9,000/£60,000 x 100 = 15%

Interpretation of ARR

- The higher the ARR the higher the return on investment.
- The ARR can be compared with the ARRs of alternative investment opportunities.

- It can also be compared with the bank rate. However it would need to be significantly higher than the interest rate in order to be worthwhile pursuing as it is a much riskier use of finance.

Net Present Value

This method of investment appraisal calculates the current value of the future expected cash flows and ensures they are higher than the initial investment. To calculate the current value of future cash flows, discounted cash flows are used.

Discounted cash flow

To discount cash flow means to take into account the interest that the money could have accumulated if it were sitting in the bank earning interest. Therefore the amount cash flows must be discounted by depends on the interest rate at the time.

The table shows an example for the potential launch of two products with a discount factor* of 4%.

The project with the highest NPV would usually be chosen. In this case product B has the higher NPV so has the higher real return.

	Launch product A			Launch product B		
	Cash flow	Discount factor*	Discounted cash flow	Cash flow	Discount factor*	Discounted cash flow
0	(£100,000)	1	(£100,000)	(£120,000)	1	(£120,000)
1	£40,000	0.96	£38,400	£40,000	0.96	£38,400
2	£40,000	0.92	£36,800	£50,000	0.92	£46,000
3	£40,000	0.89	£35,600	£60,000	0.89	£53,400
	NPV of product A		£10,800	NPV of product B		£17,800

*The calculation of the discount factors is not required by the AQA specification, so you will always be given this information in the exam.

Table 11.1 Potential launch of two products with a discount factor of 4%.

Application

In six months' time, London's best ice-cream parlour (*Scoop*) plans on opening its second outlet. It has identified one site near the tourist magnet of Carnaby Street and another in Brewer Street. The initial outlay will be twice as much for one as for the other (excuse the cageyness, but this is a true story). To decide which to go ahead with there is a need for a cool look at money in and money out. By measuring passers-by, an estimate can be made of the likely sales level at each outlet compared with the original one in Covent Garden. By forecasting cash flows for the next four years and comparing them with the initial sum put at risk, a decision can be made.

A* Insight

Most candidates can deal with the numbers in an investment appraisal question. Only the best, though, can interpret the findings effectively in relation to the objectives and the circumstances of the business in question. If the text has suggested cash flow problems, pay-back suddenly becomes the most important method of appraisal (getting your cash back as quickly as possible). Indeed, if cash is tight, can the business risk investing at all? As ever, A* candidates think about the circumstances and think for themselves.

Themes for evaluation

It is important to consider the business in question when carrying out a full investment appraisal. For example, what are the organisation's objectives? Short-term profits or long-term growth? If the focus is on the short term, then a quick payback is likely to be important. Discounted cash flows are related to longer-term investment periods.

As always when dealing with numerical data which comes from forecasts, it is important to consider the source and the likelihood of accuracy. The longer in advance that cash flows are forecasted the harder it becomes to forecast.

Also although the current interest rate is known, it could change considerably over a period of, say, five years. This could undermine the basis of the DCF method of investment appraisal. It effectively assumes a constant interest rate over a period of time.

The trade-off between risk and reward should also be considered. Some projects may have potentially high returns but also carry high risks (for example launching a new product). Whether or not a firm chooses a riskier option may depend on its current market standing, the culture of the organisation or the firm's objectives.

Test yourself (20 marks)

1   From the following cash flows, calculate which is the better investment, using payback and ARR.   (10)

	Investment A		Investment B	
	Net cash flow	Cumulative cash	Net cash flow	Cumulative cash
Now	(£80,000)		(£50,000)	
Year 1	£10,000		£0	
Year 2	£70,000		£32,000	
Year 3	£36,000		£36,000	

2   A firm is considering launching a new product. It will cost £400,000 to launch, will be priced at £2, has variable costs of £1.20 and annual fixed overheads of £60,000. Sales are forecast to be:

Year 1   200,000 units

Year 2   300,000 units

Year 3   150,000 units

Using payback and ARR, decide whether it should proceed or not.   (10)

3 Advanced marketing

Unit 12   Understanding marketing objectives

What?

A marketing objective is a marketing-related goal that must be achieved in order for an organisation to achieve its overall business objective. An example could be 'to increase market share from 22% to 25% by 2012'. Having been agreed, the objective will be fundamental to every marketing decision made by management. Even if a price increase might boost profit sharply, an objective of boosting market share will put the price rise on hold. This is because, once an overall corporate objective has been agreed, it is vital that all departments deliver on their promises. A goal of increasing market share might have led the operations department to open an extra night shift. A decision to increase price would stop the sales growth and therefore make the extra night shift redundant. The business functions have to work together – common objectives is the usual way to achieve this.

How?

Marketing objectives will usually be set by senior level management or at board director level. It may well be set by the marketing director and agreed with the rest of the board. In some circumstances the overall business objective, will, in fact be a marketing objective (e.g. increase sales/increase market share). In such a case it may be set by the managing director.

Why?

Marketing is a fundamental determinant of the long-term success of a business. Marketing objectives provide goals and, when broken down further, specific targets for the staff in the marketing department.

Which?

Marketing objectives can be broken down into four key categories:

1 **Increase product differentiation**
   This is the degree to which consumers perceive the product to be different from others on the market. The higher the degree of product differentiation:

- the less direct the competition
- the higher the degree of brand loyalty
- the lower the price elasticity of demand. This enables higher prices to be charged and higher profit margins to be made.

2 **Growth**
Growth objectives usually come in two forms:
- increase sales
- increase market share.
However they could also be:
- increase number of stores
- increase product range.
Growth is often seen as the key objective of medium and large businesses. However, it can cause problems such as cannibalisation. This occurs when growth eats into sales of existing stores/products rather than takes sales from competitors.

Application

Cannibalisation has been a problem for businesses such as Subway because one town often has more than one store. The second Subway will often steal business from the first rather than create new business for itself. The franchisee of the new store may be unconcerned about where the business is coming from, as his income depends purely on his store's performance. The Subway head office, though, would definitely not want cannibalisation to take place.

3 **Continuity**
It is important for major brands to take a long-term view. Sometimes it can be tempting to reduce prices in order to boost sales, or accept cheaper, lower quality supplies in order to boost profit margins. However, brands that expect to be around for many years should not risk damaging their reputation for the sake of short-term financial gain.

4 **Innovation**
Innovation is particularly crucial in rapidly changing markets such as the mobile phone market. Much of Nokia's success over the last 15 years can be attributed to the firm's ability to design and produce a great number of different phone designs. This has helped to keep customers interested and ensure there is always a new product for teenagers to want and the rich to have.

A* Insight

Most candidates accept a firm's marketing objectives uncritically. They assume that the firm knows what it is doing. A top student will always question and criticise. For example, what if Pepsi set the objective of becoming the Number 1 cola? A wise student would cast doubt on this. Outselling Coca-Cola? I don't think so.

Constraints

A constraint is a factor that may prevent a firm from achieving its objectives. The factor could be internal to the organisation or external.

External constraints include:

- **Competition** – Mars may set a goal of boosting sales of its Galaxy milk chocolate from 5% to 7% of the UK market; but remember that a market share increase from 5% to 7% means a 40% (two fifths) sales increase. Most of that would have to come from sales of Cadbury's Dairy Milk. Cadbury would not allow this to happen without putting up a huge fight.
- **Consumer tastes** – When fashion turns against you, it is hard to turn the tide. French Connection's 'FCUK' logo made it a super-hot brand until people went off it in late 2006. In the years that followed, French Connection launched some great collections of clothes, but sales kept sliding.
- **Economic variables** – The dramatic 2008/09 slide in sales of items from houses to cars to restaurant meals showed that, at times, economic forces can sweep aside a company's own plans; optimistic goals had to be ignored as survival became the key objective.
- **Legal** – The Cadbury salmonella case is a reminder that firms forget about consumer safety and protection at their peril. Many years ago the customer was the one to suffer; today big firms can suffer if they end up in court.

Internal constraints:

- **Financial** – Can the business afford to spend enough to achieve the marketing objectives?
- **Personnel** – Does the business have the right people with the right skills and motivation for the task?
- **Market position** – It may be that the strength of the firm's market position makes it hard to break out of the consumer's image; for example could Marmite make chewing gum, would people trust Heinz to make a good curry?

Application

In 2007 Cadbury was taken to court by Birmingham City Council. It was being prosecuted for safety breaches that led to an outbreak of salmonella food poisoning. The prosecutor accused the confectionery giant of seeking to cut costs and reduce wastage with a 'tolerance level' for salmonella in its products. This extraordinary action led to more than 1 million bars having to be recalled and some dreadful publicity that resulted in a slippage in market share. Cadbury was later fined £1 million and also apologised for its actions.

Themes for evaluation

It is vital for a firm to have clear objectives as without objectives the firm may lack direction, focus and cohesiveness. It is important that everyone in the organisation is working towards the same goal.

Marketing objectives are important as they enable strategies to be devised. From here more specific targets and plans of action can be drawn up.

In order to evaluate a firm's marketing objectives it is important to look at them alongside the corporate objective. Does the marketing objective help the firm to achieve its overall goal?

Constraints are also a useful avenue for evaluation. Judgement can be drawn by looking at how likely the firm is to achieve its objectives given the constraints it is up against.

Test yourself (15 marks)

1 What is meant by a marketing objective? (3)
2 State two benefits of increasing product differentiation. (2)
3 Explain why increasing market share and increasing sales are not necessarily the same thing. (4)
4 State two benefits of ensuring continuity. (2)
5 Assume McDonald's marketing objective is to increase sales. Explain two possible constraints they may come up against. (4)

Unit 13 Analysing markets

What?

What is meant by the term 'market' in this context is the consumers or potential consumers. Therefore it is the customers that we are analysing. This may include:

- the number of customers
- whether and to what extent this number is growing or shrinking
- what the buying habits of these customers are
- how these buying habits might be changing.

Why?

The fundamental goal of market analysis is to gain a better understanding of the market. This might lead to an improvement in the product range on offer (and therefore higher sales) or identify a completely new market opportunity. This is something that should be done before a product is launched onto the market and regularly afterwards, to keep up with changing consumer tastes and – perhaps – competitors' bright new ideas.

Application

Bright entrepreneurs in America have developed a 'probiotic' pizza. The plan is to achieve in the takeaway food market what Danone has managed in the yoghurt/dessert market. Products such as Activia are bought because people think they are healthier than rival brands ('good for the gut'). Just conceivably, some in America may secretly hope that 'good for the gut' means losing weight. If so, the new Naked Pizza stands to make a fortune. The founders realise that people want to eat a full-on pizza with tasty toppings – but would also love to believe it's going to make their tums happier.

Which?

1. **Consumer usage and attitudes** – Consumer usage refers to how often, when and how consumers use products. Knowing, for example, that 80% of consumers use the product with friends may influence both the product development and the promotion.
2. **Consumer profiles** – this refers to the statistical breakdown of the characteristics of people who buy a particular product. Characteristics to be analysed include: age, income, gender, social class, region, occupation and interests. This analysis can be useful as it may highlight particular ways to promote, distribute or modify a product in order to best appeal to consumers.
3. **Market mapping** –
Market mapping involves:
   - selecting two key market factors, e.g. price and usage
   - plotting the position of key brands on a market map.

Market map for chocolate based on luxury/everyday and filling/light snack

The construction of a market map enables potential gaps in the market to be spotted. In this case there may be room in the market for a high priced chocolate. However, whether such a product is a realistic addition to the market is another matter!

Why?

The Need to Forecast Sales

Launching a new product such as a new cosmetic or new chocolate bar is likely to cost at least £10 million. No less importantly, a company such as Cadbury will make its new bar the key sales target for its sales force, i.e. their focus is taken off other brands as they push hard on the new one. This means that Cadbury are not just investing £10 million, they stand to lose out on sales backing for other products, i.e. there is an opportunity cost to every new product launch. It is awful, therefore, to put lots of money and effort into a new brand that proves to be a dog even before making it to the giddy heights of a problem child. Carefully researching a new product idea should help separate good ideas from weaker ones. Then quantitative research on a large sample should be able to lead to a sales forecast. Sadly, the awful track record of many top consumer goods firms shows that it still isn't easy.

How?

Test markets: market research is used widely, but as only one in six new products succeeds in the marketplace, it is clear that firms struggle to be sure which new product ideas are good ones. To help answer this, firms can use a test market. This means going through a real product launch, but only in a small area – perhaps a town or, more likely, a region, e.g. the North-East.

Test markets show real people going into real shops and making real purchasing decisions. For the producer, the key is to see how many people try and – especially – repeat-purchase the product. After all, if a new chocolate bar comes out, lots of us are happy to buy it once or twice. The problem is that most people soon revert to their old favourites. A three-month test market is expensive to run, but will answer most of the questions about the product's likely success or failure.

Extrapolation of trends: this technique is the way firms forecast the sales of their existing products. This is needed because every business function needs to know what sales are likely to be in six or 12 months' time. Operations need to know whether extra production capacity is needed (time to move to a bigger factory?) and HR needs to know whether they are hiring or firing in the coming months. Look at the graph below. It plots actual sales for the first 16 months of a firm's life. Then finds the line of best fit to extrapolate the trend forwards. This suggests that the business had better be prepared for £140,000 plus of sales in the coming October. Can it cope? The answer, of course, is that it's much easier to cope if you are prepared.

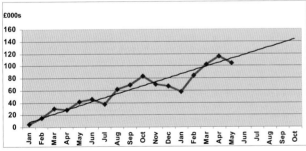

Figure 13.2 Newbie's monthly sales to date (May, Year 2)

Moving averages: an alternative way to extrapolate is to calculate the moving average within a set of data. Then it's possible to forecast coming months or years on the basis of the data. The value of a moving average is that it gives a good sense of the trend without eliminating the sense that sales are fluctuating. In other words, whereas the line of best fit (in the graph) shows a single straight line, moving averages smooth out individual months, yet still show ups and downs within the trend. This is shown in the graph below:

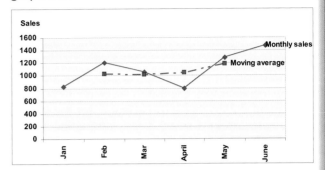

Figure 13.3 Establishing the trend using a moving average

Application

In order to gain key application marks various aspects of the business in question can be considered:
- Is it new or well-established? The more established the organisation the more likely the firm is to understand its market.
- How competitive is the market? The more fierce the competition the more important it is to understand the market.

Themes for evaluation

- Judgements have to be made about the importance of findings. Some findings may be hugely useful (e.g. 80% of customers buy the product on impulse) whereas other findings may not be particularly enlightening (e.g. 40% of consumers eat the product at home compared to 60% who eat it outside of the home).
- Market analysis can be crucial in fiercely competitive markets as knowledge is power. The more the firm knows about its consumers the better it may be able to satisfy them.

Test yourself (20 marks)

1 Why might effective market analysis be more important to business success than effective sales promotion? (4)
2 Why may it prove a mistake to start a business where there is a gap that can be identified in a market map? (4)
3 Outline two reasons why a test market might be more effective than a market research survey. (4)
4 How might a firm's finance department make use of extrapolated sales figures for the coming year? (4)
5 Briefly explain why extrapolated figures might prove incorrect. (4)

Unit 14 Measuring and forecasting trends

What?

A trend is the general direction of data over a period of time. For example, the British economy has grown at a rate of 2.25% a year (on average) for the last 50 years. Forecasting a trend means estimating future values. When a business first starts, forecasting is hugely difficult because there may be little or no data on which to base estimates.

Why?

Managers need to be able to anticipate what may happen in the future in order to prepare for it. For example, if sales of Oishii Sushi follow the trend shown in the graph below:

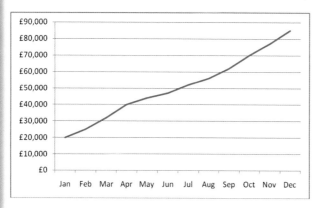

Figure 14.1 Oishii Sushi sales graph

It may be important that managers estimate future sales values so they can ensure they:
- order the right quantity of stock for the coming month
- employ and train the right number of staff for the next three to six months
- invest in the right level of capacity for the next six to 12 months.

Which?

Moving averages

A moving average is an average for consecutive periods of time. For example, look at how the three month moving average shows the steady trend in sales in the following table:

Month	Sales	3-month total	3-month moving average
January	10,000	N/A	N/A
February	10,000	N/A	N/A
March	13,000	33,000	11,000
April	12,000	35,000	11,667
May	14,000	39,000	13,000
June	15,000	41,000	13,667
July	16,000	45,000	15,000
August	20,000	51,000	17,000

Reasons to use moving averages:
1 Sales may vary wildly from one month to the next (often the case in the early stages of a product launch). As they may seem to follow a random pattern from one month to the next, calculating the moving average makes it easier to see underlying trends.
2 This is also a particularly useful technique to use when sales depend heavily on seasonal variations. For example, ice cream, hot chocolate or smoothie sales. Again it helps to spot the underlying trend.

Key point: Three-month moving averages help to reveal underlying trends.

Extrapolation

This means to make a prediction on the future, based on past data. Take the table below as an example.

Month	Sales revenue
January	£2,000
February	£4,000
March	£6,000
April	£8,000
May	£10,000
June	£12,000
July	?
August	?

As sales have been steadily rising each month, it would be reasonable to assume that they will continue to do so in the following months. Using extrapolation, one would expect July sales to be £14,000 and August sales to be £16,000.

This is often done by continuing a line on a graph to extend the current trend. It can also be done by looking at a set of numbers and estimating the next value/values in the set.

Problems with extrapolation

This technique is based on the assumption that underlying trends in the market will not change. In reality that is rarely true for long periods of time. External factors will affect the market in the future; and the further ahead the forecast is looking, the more inaccurate it is likely to prove. Factors that can cause dramatic changes include:

1 **Social factors** – changing of consumer tastes and attitudes.
2 **Economic factors** – changing interest rates, income levels, exchange rates and the economic cycle.
3 **Competition** – changes in the number of competitors, quality of substitutes and price of substitutes.

Correlation

This considers how one variable will affect another (often sales).

For example:
- How do changes in the amount spent on advertising affect sales?
- How do changes in the economy affect labour turnover?
- How do changes in price affect sales?

The three key factors to consider:

1 Is there a relationship between the two variables? If so, is this relationship positive or negative?
2 How strong is the relationship between the two variables?
3 Is the relationship causal? I.e. is the one trend definitely a cause of the other?

Consider the graph below. It shows sales plotted alongside spending on advertising.

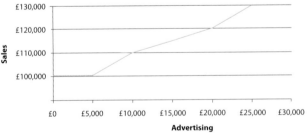

From looking at the graph above, it is clear that advertising has a strong positive correlation with sales. As the advertising increases, the sales increase. However, it is important to remember that from these numbers one does not actually know that the reason for the increase in sales is the increase in advertising. Many factors could have combined to produce this effect. For example:

- changes in consumer tastes
- changes in population
- changes in quality of product
- changes in price/quality of substitute products.

Key terms

Correlation – when one series of numerical data seems related to another series, whether positively or negatively.
Extrapolation – continuing a statistical trend into the future, either using a graph or calculations.
Moving average – a way to smooth an erratic series of data, to help see the underlying trend.

Exam insight

Extrapolation is a widely used way to attempt to forecast the future, but often proves laughably wrong. Similarly, correlation can easily be misinterpreted. Each year Chanel spends millions in December advertising its No. 5 perfume. And, each year, sales shoot ahead in December. But are the extra sales because of the advertising? Surely the extra sales are because of Christmas. And because of the extra sales in the perfume market, Chanel chooses to advertise in December. In this case, then, the causal relationship is unclear. In exams, always be sceptical about jumping to conclusions. And, in case studies, be wary of managers who treat statistics with simplistic enthusiasm.

Themes for evaluation

The accuracy of forecasted data depends on:
- The source of the information. If it is gathered by an owner with a particular motive he or she may overstate values in order to gain investment/authorisation for a project.
- The length of time into the future with which data is being forecasted. The longer the period of time the more difficult it is to forecast accurately. Figures for the next three months should be reasonably accurate but figures forecast years into the future may well be way off.
- The market conditions. When the market is fairly stable it is easier to forecast data accurately than it is in times of considerable changes in the market or the economy.

Test yourself (15 marks)

1 Why is it important to accurately forecast sales? (5)
2 What is extrapolation? (2)
3 Why might it be useful for a firm to know the correlation between advertising and sales? (4)
4 What are the problems with relying on correlation figures? (4)

Unit 15 Selecting marketing strategies

What?

A marketing strategy is a carefully considered plan of the marketing activity required in order for the corporate objectives to be met. A good marketing strategy will take advantage of a firm's differentiators and bear in mind the length and stage of the product life cycle.

Application

The strategy supporting Heinz Beans will bear in mind that the brand is in its maturity stage – more than 100 years after its birth – and probably has at least another hundred years of profitable sales to come. A suitable strategy would have a timescale of three to 10 years. By contrast, the marketing for a computer game will aim to have maximum impact within a timescale of perhaps now to three months' time. When thinking about marketing strategy, think carefully about the specific circumstances of the business and its brands.

In order to select the best strategy, it is important to consider:

- company objectives
- finance available
- potential rewards
- the context of the business and its brands.

Why?

Marketing strategies are important because they outline exactly what marketing activities need to be done in order for key objectives to be met. The strategies can then be broken down into individual or group action plans and targets. These can help to give employees clear direction, focus and motivation.

The difference between marketing strategy and marketing tactics

A strategy is a medium to long-term plan of action which is expected to have long-term benefits whereas a tactic is a quick action with short-term implications.

For example:
Marketing tactic – cut price by 10p for launch of product.

Marketing strategy – reduce the price of an aging luxury mobile phone from a premium to competitive price in order to target the mass market.

Which?

Types of strategy

Ansoff's matrix

Ansoff's matrix is a diagram which shows how new a product is and how new the market that it is entering is. This shows how the degree of risk rises as the knowledge of product and market falls.

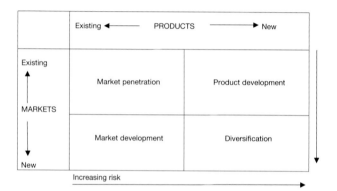

Market penetration

This means to concentrate on existing products in existing markets in order to develop market share. This is the least risky strategy as both the market and the product are familiar and understood. Although it's low risk, the rewards from success may also be low; existing customers within a market develop regular shopping habits, therefore it's difficult and expensive to, for example, shift a consumer from their Galaxy chocolate habit to a Yorkie one.

Market development

This means to still concentrate on existing products but to develop or find new markets in which to sell them. It could involve targeting the product at new segments of the market or to different areas of the country or even different countries. An example is Cadbury's launch of Dairy Milk in China.

Product development

This means to remain in the same market but develop new products to be sold within that market.

Examples could include Coca-Cola's release of Coke Zero. This strategy is riskier than market penetration and possibly even riskier than market development as the vast majority of new products do not succeed. Also launching new products often requires huge investments of time, money and resources.

Diversification

This means to launch a new product into a new market. This is the riskiest type of strategy as it involves moving into an unknown market with an unknown product. Although it is hugely risky, the result of successful diversification is to reduce a company's dependence on one market and one product. Diversification is risky to do, but can result in a less risky business. A moderate example of diversification is Coca-Cola's launch of Relentless into the energy drink/nightclub sector dominated by Red Bull. A more dramatic example is Nintendo's move from producing packs of cards into the electronic games industry.

Diversification reduces a firm's dependence on particular markets. If a business only sells chocolate and some government research is released which shows chocolate to be linked with a particularly dangerous illness, that firm will be seriously affected. If a business has a portfolio of different products including chocolate, changes to this market will be less damaging for them.

Remember strategies should:
- contribute to achieving overall company objectives
- be looking to the future
- be considered with great care
- find the best fit between company objectives, resources available to the firm and the opportunities within the market
- set out exactly which activities will be done and when.

Key terms

Ansoff's matrix – a grid showing whether the strategy is rooted in existing or new products and markets; and therefore the risks and rewards involved.
Diversification – moving into a new market with a new product, and therefore taking on huge risks in the hope of huge rewards.
Strategy – a medium to long-term plan which is implemented in order to help a firm achieve its objective.
Tactics – a quick action that tends to have a short-term effect. For example, if Debenhams decide to have a four day pre-Christmas sale where all products are 20% off, this will increase short-term sales but is unlikely to have any longer term effect on the business.

Themes for evaluation

Working in marketing is interesting because there are no magic formulas. The same marketing director might come up with a great strategy one year, but the wrong one next time around. Markets never stay the same – customer tastes and habits change, often in response to changes in the economy. Every large business uses market research extensively before devising a strategy – but mistakes can still be made. If the business culture is risk-averse, a cautious marketing director will adopt a safety-first marketing strategy (probably: 'let's do the same as last year'). This can lead companies to spend too long following a path that is heading for a dead end (such as Kodak, which kept pursuing film until its market was swept away by digital cameras). Success in marketing strategy may require boldness. The best strategy might echo the words of *Star Trek*: 'To boldy go where no man has gone before'.

A* insight

Ansoff's matrix is about the relationship between risk and reward associated with different business strategies. The example of Nintendo is perfect to illustrate this. How likely was it that a small producer of playing cards would end up beating the mammoth Sony (PS3) and Microsoft (Xbox 360) in the games console business? Yet despite the risks, the rewards have been vast. Playing cards now account for less than 1% of Nintendo's business – and Nintendo's profits regularly outstrip Sony's.

Yet most students see Ansoff as purely to do with risk; they forget the other side – reward. Therefore your answers can stand out if you analyse both sides of the theory.

Test yourself (20 marks)

1 What is a marketing strategy? (3)
2 What is the difference between a strategy and a tactic? (3)
3 What can Ansoff's matrix be used for? (6)
4 Explain the following:
   a) Market penetration
   b) Market development
   c) Product development
   d) Diversification. (8)

 **Unit 16** Developing and implementing marketing plans

What?

A **marketing plan** is a document detailing how a firm's marketing strategy will be turned into marketing actions. It should include the following elements:
- An overview of the plan.
- The corporate and marketing objectives.
- The marketing strategies that will be carried out in order to ensure the objectives are met.
- Specific marketing activities including market analysis, advertising, PR and sales promotions.
- A detailed budget. This would consist of a breakdown of all expected expenditures and revenues on marketing activities.
- A monitoring plan. A detailed plan for how the strategies and budget will be monitored to ensure budgets are adhered to and targets are met.

Why?

A marketing plan helps a business bring its marketing activities together as an integrated plan rather that a set of stand-alone activities. For example, because TV advertising is very expensive, many firms combine a smallish TV campaign with advertising on poster hoardings plus advertising in-store. The idea is that the TV commercial triggers your interest, the poster reminds you and the in-store material directs you to the product. A marketing plan will help make sure that all these things happen at the same time. Otherwise the company's budget will be wasted.

Other benefits of a marketing plan are:
- clearly outlines which activities will be carried out, when and by whom
- it may help a business prepare for potential problems
- it should give staff a clear idea of how the marketing activities fit in with the overall business objectives
- enables success to be measured.

Which?

Factors which must be considered when drawing up a marketing plan

1 Setting a marketing budget

It is hard for any business to be sure what the 'right' amount of money is to be spent on marketing. Part of the problem is summed up in the famous saying (usually attributed to Lord Leverhulme of Unilever): 'I know half my advertising money is wasted. The problem is I don't know which half'. In 2009 Unilever spent more than £5,000 million worldwide on advertising and promotions, so the wasted half accounts for £2.5 billion!

What if Unilever decided to increase its **marketing budget** by half, to £7.5 billion? Clearly it could only afford to do that if it anticipated sales increases high enough to generate more than £2.5 billion of extra gross profit. The problem is how could anyone be sure that this would happen? Unilever will suspect that if it increases the marketing spending on its brands such as Persil, PG Tips and Timotei, its big rival Procter & Gamble will respond. Then the extra spending will tend to cancel itself out, leaving the TV companies better off, but Unilever and Procter & Gamble worse off.

There are two common ways to set a marketing budget:
- Matched to the objectives, i.e. to make an estimate of the sum of money required to make the marketing objectives achievable. If Cadbury wants to boost its share of the chocolate market from 32% to 34%, the marketing director will warn that this will be expensive. If £50 million was spent last year in Britain, it may be that £65–£75 million would be needed this year to achieve that level of sales growth (remember, chocolate is a very mature market, and customers are set in their ways). The finance director can then advise the board on whether this is worthwhile.
- Matched to the competition, i.e. to spend enough to communicate to customers above the 'noise' put out by your competitors. If easyJet spends £5 million on advertising every week in *The Sun*, Ryanair will almost certainly start doing the same.

Application

In September 2009 the advertising account for Moneysupermarket.com was switched to a new advertising agency. The £14 million advertising campaign featuring 'Dragon' Peter Jones had not been working. It was being outshone by that of rival Comparethemarket.com, which starred a meerkat (a furry animal). During 2008 and 2009 four companies had been fighting hard to stand out in the online price comparison market: GoCompare, Moneysupermarket,

Comparethemarket and Confused. Each needed a big enough budget to keep its name 'alive'. In the short term, most of the profit in the sector was sucked away by 'overspending' on TV advertising. But without this spending, any one of the four brands would lose recognition and fade away.

Other factors affecting the size of a marketing budget include:
- The objectives of the organisation.
- The nature of the product and the importance of that product to the firm.
- The stage of the life cycle of the product – or the phase within the Boston Matrix, i.e. a cash cow will have relatively little spent on it, whereas a rising star may be given massive support.

A* insight

Top students will never forget Lord Leverhulme's famous saying: 'Developing a marketing plan is easy. Developing a successful one is surprisingly difficult.'

2 Constraints
Constraints are factors that may prevent the firm from meeting its objectives.
Internal constraints include:
Finance
- How much is available?
- When is it likely to be available?
- How much revenue must an activity generate in order to be deemed successful?

Operations
- Is there enough stock available?
- How quickly can production be increased?
- Is there the factory space to hold extra raw materials?
- Is there the warehouse space to hold extra finished goods?

HR
- Are there enough staff to deal with additional demand?
- Do those staff have the right skills and attitudes to deal with extra demand?

External constraints include:
- How will competitors respond?
- Could a price cut result in a price war?
- What follow-up marketing is expected from competitors?
- Are the marketing goals realistic given the state of the economy?

3 Monitoring performance
This aspect of the plan is almost the most important as it should help to improve marketing decisions in future. By carefully monitoring the relative success of marketing activities a firm can get a clearer idea

of what works and what doesn't for its products. As mentioned above, Moneysupermarket.com switched its advertising agency because of disappointing results from its advertising campaign. Regular monitoring gives a better chance of finding out which is the wasted half of the money the firm is spending.

Application

The relative importance of a marketing plan depends on certain aspects of the business in question.
1 **The market** – In a rapidly changing market it may be more important to get new products to the market quickly due to first-mover advantages, than it is to ensure the marketing is clearly defined and structured.
2 **The size of the firm** – Although all firms may benefit from doing a detailed plan of marketing activities, smaller firms are less likely to have the resources, knowledge or personnel to do this effectively.
3 **The nature of the industry** – In consumer markets, marketing tends to be of vital importance, whereas in industrial markets marketing tends to be less important.

Key terms

Marketing budget – the sum of money set aside for spending on marketing activities.
Marketing plan – the document setting out which marketing activities will be done and when.

Themes for evaluation

Marketing plans can help a business to clarify its objectives, set targets and timelines. However they might also stifle creativity and flair if the marketing plan is stuck to very rigidly. Bright tactical ideas can help boost sales, but employees might learn to keep them to themselves if they fall outside the lines of the plan.

Great marketing often comes from instinct or a hunch rather than careful planning. Therefore it is important that plans have the flexibility to allow great ideas to bypass the bureaucracy and be transformed into action quickly and effectively.

Test yourself (20 marks)

1 What is a marketing plan? (3)
2 State two benefits of constructing a marketing plan. (2)
3 Outline two potential external constraints. (4)
4 Outline two potential internal constraints. (4)
5 Explain why monitoring the performance of marketing activities is important. (7)

4 Advanced people in organisations

Unit 17 Key AS people issues

Introduction

'Human Resource Strategies' is a key section of your A2 Business Studies course. According to the AQA specification: 'This section considers the strategies available to businesses in managing their human resources. It builds upon AS Human Resource materials.'

So you need a thorough understanding of the people issues studied at AS in order to understand, analyse and evaluate these new A2 theories properly.

Organisational structures

When faced with an A2 case study, one of the first things you should do is to quickly identify and assess the firm's organisational structure and the job roles carried out by key employees. It is helpful to do this before you begin to consider your answers, even if none of the exam questions seems to require it. This is because the organisational structure of a business has a major impact on communication and employee participation within a business, on its levels of efficiency and, ultimately, on its ability to compete and respond to change.

The examiner will expect good A2 candidates to draw on their AS understanding by expressing ideas using relevant terms, such as *layers of hierarchy*, *span of control* and *delegation*. Being able to examine the impact of changes to the existing organisational structure will help to demonstrate your skills of analysis and evaluation. Valuable marks can also be earned if you can interpret any human resources data provided by applying one or more measures of workforce performance (see below). This enables you to make informed comments about the firm's performance and what could be done to improve it.

For example:
- Falling rates of productivity are likely to lead to higher costs, resulting in a loss of competitiveness if the business is forced to increase prices or cut back on investment.
- Increasing labour turnover is often seen as an indication of low staff morale, perhaps due to a change in working conditions, and can also mean higher costs for the business.

Recruiting, selecting and training employees

At AS level, you learned how businesses tried to get the best employees via the process of recruitment and methods of training. You will be required to use this knowledge at A2 to comment on the human resource strategies and workforce planning of the case study business. You will need to be able to assess the extent to which these plans are helping the business to achieve its strategic objectives (or, indeed, preventing it from doing so). Good A2 students will understand the benefits of creating and maintaining a highly-skilled workforce, but also recognise that it can be a costly process to do so.

Motivating employees

Your AS course will have developed your understanding of a range of methods – both financial and non-financial – to motivate employees to work more effectively, as well as a number of theories of motivation, such as Herzberg's 'two factor theory' or Maslow's 'hierarchy of needs'. You will not be questioned specifically about any of this in either of your A2 examinations. However, motivation is still a key issue. Changes to existing levels of motivation

Measure	Meaning	Formula
Labour productivity	Measures the efficiency in terms of the level of output produced per unit of input (usually workers).	$\dfrac{\text{Total output}}{\text{Number of workers}}$
Labour turnover	Measures the number of staff that leave a firm over a given period of time.	$\dfrac{\text{Staff leavers over one year}}{\text{Average number employed}} \times 100$

Table 17.1: Key measures of workforce performance

can have a huge impact on a firm's ability to control costs, quality and wastage levels, affecting its ability to compete against rivals. In particular, you should make sure that you can use relevant theories and methods to:

- identify and explain the reasons behind current human resource problems, such as deteriorating employer-employee relations
- explore possible solutions to human resource issues such as low productivity.

Exam insight ....

It is important to remember that the A2 section of your A level is one half of a whole – you need, therefore, to bring all of your AS knowledge with you in order to progress successfully. Examiners often remark that A2 answers about personnel issues are overly focused on motivation, to the exclusion of other factors. Beware of this.

Your A2 examinations will be much more demanding and expect you to use your knowledge – both old and new – selectively to analyse and evaluate.

Key terms

Communication – the exchange of information between individuals or groups, either within the business (internal) or to those outside of the business (external).

Delayering – the removal of one or more layers of management within a business, usually to reduce overheads.

Delegation – the passing of authority down the hierarchy from managers to subordinates (more junior employees).

Empowerment – involves giving employees further down the hierarchy more control over their working lives, by allowing them to plan and regulate the work they do, as well as carry it out.

Hierarchy – the internal structure of an organisation, often shown as a diagram known as an organisational chart, indicating who is responsible for and accountable to whom.

Layers of hierarchy – the number of levels making up a firm's organisational structure, from senior directors down to shop-floor workers.

Motivation – the desire to work, which, according to theorists such as Herzberg, comes from within, rather than from extrinsic rewards such as pay.

Span of control – the number of subordinates for which a manager is directly responsible.

Test yourself (50 marks)

1 Describe what is meant by the terms a) span of control and b) chain of command. (2)
2 State two differences between a tall organisation and a flat organisation. (3)
3 Outline two reasons why a business might choose to remove one or more layers from its hierarchy. (2)
4 Explain two negative consequences for a firm carrying out a process of delayering. (3)
5 Identify two benefits to a firm of training its managers to delegate successfully. (2)
6 State two factors that can influence whether or not delegation can be successfully introduced. (2)
7 Explain one key difference between a director and a manager within a large business. (2)
8 Outline two causes of falling labour productivity. (2)
9 Briefly examine two negative consequences of a sudden and unexpected rise in labour turnover. (4)
10 State two reasons why a business might choose to recruit new staff. (2)
11 Examine one reason why a rapidly growing business might choose to recruit externally, rather than internally. (3)
12 Outline one benefit and one cost of training to a firm in a highly competitive market. (3)
13 Describe one advantage of a) on the job training, b) off the job training. (2)
14 Briefly analyse one benefit to a business of having a highly-motivated workforce. (2)
15 Using examples, briefly explain the difference between a hygiene factor and a genuine motivator, according to Herzberg's two-factor theory of motivation. (3)
16 Using examples, explain the difference between lower order needs and higher order needs, according to Maslow's hierarchy. (3)
17 Give two examples of fringe benefits. (2)
18 Briefly explain the difference between performance-related pay and profit sharing. (3)
19 State two methods of job enlargement. (2)
20 Use one theory of motivation to briefly explain why working in teams can increase motivation. (3)

Managing people – what does it involve?

Human resource management (HRM) means devising and implementing policies to manage a firm's workforce effectively. The major issue relating to HRM is whether the function is treated sufficiently seriously by the directors to ensure that it is represented at board level. In many companies, the HR 'Director' is not actually a member of the board. So whereas Marketing, Finance and Operations are represented at all the key decision-making meetings, HR may not be.

Whether or not HR is represented at board level, its areas of responsibility can be defined quite clearly:
- **Workforce planning** – identifies a firm's future employee requirements in relation to its corporate objectives (e.g. increased market share, overseas expansion, cost reduction) and compares this to the current workforce, including its size and range of skills. From here, plans can be developed to try to match the supply of labour to the demand.
- **Suitable reward systems** – the methods of remuneration chosen by a business can have a significant influence on the behaviour of employees and also on its labour costs.
- **Appropriate training programmes** – effective training should create or develop the skills required by the firm. However, training will be subject to financial constraints – although it may be highly desirable, it may be beyond the limits of a firm's training budget.
- **Effective communications** – most businesses will use a range of methods, depending on the nature of the information and its intended destination, to inform staff of management decisions, but also possibly to consult with them before decisions are made.

Any decisions taken in relation to these HRM activities will depend on the overall objectives of the business. For example, an expanding firm will have a very different approach to its workforce planning, training, etc. than a firm beginning a programme of cutbacks.

A* insight

HR professionals like to think they make important contributions to corporate strategy. This will rarely be the case if the function is not represented on the board of directors.

Who is responsible for HRM?

The responsibility for managing human resources within a business may lie with:
- **Line managers** – managers within areas such as marketing, operations and finance may have the authority to make HR decisions regarding the staff within their departments. This means that decision-makers should have an in-depth understanding of what is required. It is also the most likely approach for firms lacking the financial resources or the scale of operations required to justify using specialist HR staff (see below).
- **A human resources department** – larger businesses have more employees to plan for and more people issues to resolve, so may use specialist HR teams to help manage human resources. They also act as advisors on employment law and HR best practice.

HRM objectives

The central aim of HRM should be to maximise the contribution made by employees to the achievement of the organisation's overall objectives.

The specific HR objectives chosen to do this may relate to:
- **The level of staffing and skills required** – when a firm makes a major change such as switching from retail to online distribution, HR will need to ensure that the business has the right number of staff, with the right skills, at the right time.
- **Cost targets** – labour costs depend on the strategy adopted by the business; HR expenditure needs to be monitored against set budgets to ensure value for money.
- **Employer/employee relations** – which affects staff commitment, motivation levels and the degree of willingness to support change. Maintaining or improving these relations requires effective communication. Staff must also feel well-treated and may expect to be involved in the decision-making process.

HR strategies: soft and hard?

The attitudes and approaches of managers towards employees can vary significantly:

	Hard HRM	Soft HRM
Pros	• Quicker and easier to increase or decrease the size of the workforce, as necessary. • Speedier decision-making, as managers do not need to consult workers. • Easier to predict production outcomes, as workers' activities are tightly controlled.	• Drawing on a wider range of employees' skills and experiences may mean more creativity and innovation. • Employee consultation and increased control can improve motivation. • Management support may reduce labour turnover and absenteeism rates.
Cons	• Low levels of employee motivation, due to a lack of control over their working lives. • High levels of labour turnover, increasing recruitment costs and disrupting production. • Increased risk of mistakes because of an over-reliance on senior management.	• High levels of training will increase short-term costs and reduce productivity. • Regular consultation can slow down decision-making and lead to inflexibility. • Soft HRM may imply HR managers care more about staff than profits; this might be seen as a disadvantage.

Table 18.1 Hard HRM v soft HRM – key advantages and disadvantages

- **Hard HRM** – employees are seen as one of many inputs into the production process, generating an unwelcome but necessary cost for the business. Managers act as the decision-makers, instructing and monitoring subordinates. Jobs are broken down, giving workers little control and making them easy to replace when necessary. This approach fits in with McGregor's Theory X.
- **Soft HRM** – employees are seen as having the potential to add a great deal of value to a business, by developing their skills, abilities and interests. Managers support workers to do their jobs effectively, by providing encouragement and training, helping them to progress. This approach reflects McGregor's Theory Y.

Themes for evaluation

Ultimately, the HR objectives and strategies adopted by a business must be linked to and support the achievement of its overall objectives and strategies. A firm that is considering major expansion in the medium term will have a very different approach to one that needs to downsize its operations to reduce costs as quickly as possible in order to survive!

Exam insight ·····························

The key issue with HR objectives is who set them and how? Were they, in effect, passed down to the HR department after the directors had made the key decision ('we're closing the Coventry factory'). Or was the Head of HR an important part of the decision making process? If the HR department is just clearing up after the directors' decisions, it should not kid itself about a strategic role. A* candidates look critically at the reality of the business case.

The HRM approach adopted by a firm will largely depend on:
- the leadership style and experiences of its managers
- the attitude of its workers and the nature of the activities they are expected to carry out.

Key terms

Hard HRM – where human resources are treated in the same way as any other business resource by managers, to be hired and fired according to the firm's needs.

Line manager – managers with direct authority over and responsibility for employees within a given area of the business.

Human resource management – the business function concerned with using and developing an organisation's workforce in the most productive way to achieve overall objectives.

Soft HRM – where human resources are seen as having the potential to add great value to the business, meaning their welfare and development are considered carefully.

Test yourself (20 marks)

1   Identify two areas of a business that could have responsibility for human resource management. (2)
2   Explain two key influences on recent workforce planning carried out by car manufacturer, Toyota. (4)
3   Analyse two likely human resource objectives for budget airline Ryanair. (6)
4   State two key differences between hard and soft HRM. (2)
5   Examine two key influences on the decision by a leading car insurance company to adopt a hard approach to managing staff within its national call centre. (6)

Unit 19 Developing and implementing workforce plans

Introduction

A workforce plan aims to ensure a business has the right number of workers with the right skills and abilities to meet its present and future needs. Workforce planning is essential in helping firms to identify trends and predict necessary changes to its human resource requirements.

Components of a workforce plan

The workforce planning process aims to identify the following key pieces of information:

- The firm's corporate objectives and the implications of these for the firm's human resources.
- An estimate of the likely size of the firm's workforce and its quality (in terms of skills, abilities and attitudes) in the short, medium and long term – taking into account the effects of factors such as retirement and internal promotions.
- A forecast of the likely future demand for workers, both in terms of numbers and their skills and abilities – based on any planned changes to the firm's product portfolio and the forecast level of demand.
- A comparison of the current workforce with estimates of future needs, in order to identify any changes required.
- An examination of the external labour market in the short, medium and long term in order to make judgements on the availability of appropriately skilled staff.
- Recommendations regarding the policies needed to address future human resource needs, including recruitment, training, redeployment and/or redundancy.

Influences on workforce plans

Managers will need to consider a number of factors that can have a significant influence on their ability to produce accurate forecasts of the likely supply of and demand for labour:

Internal influences

Factors from within the business include:

- **Corporate strategies** – a business aiming to expand via organic growth will have very different human resource requirements to one that takes over or merges with a rival.
- **Operational strategies** – the nature of a firm's products, the scale of its operations and the production methods used will have a major influence on the number of workers and the skills they need to possess.
- **Marketing strategies** – the marketing plans developed to support the achievement of corporate objectives will also impact on human resources.
- **Financial constraints** – all businesses, regardless of size, will set budgets limiting levels of expenditure on areas such as recruitment, training, pay levels, etc., in order to control costs and operate as efficiently as possible.

External influences

Factors from outside of the business include:

- **Sales forecasts** – businesses are more likely to recruit more workers if sales are predicted to rise. Falling sales may not automatically trigger redundancies, but may mean that those employees that do leave are not replaced, or that training programmes are postponed.
- **Labour market conditions** – a shortage of young workers resulting from raising the school leaving age to 18 could push up wage rates, encouraging firms to recruit retired people.
- **Developments in technology** – technological change leads to new products and production processes, creating a need to recruit (or retrain) workers with the necessary skills.
- **Changes in legislation** – changes to existing employment, equal opportunity and health and safety legislation can have significant effects on costs. For example, new legislation reducing the length of the working week could encourage firms to use more machinery, rather than increase the number of workers employed.

Implementation – key issues

- **Employer/employee relations** – significant changes to the structure of the workforce, particularly in the case of increasing workloads or compulsory redundancies, may be met with resistance and industrial action. However, regular consultation between managers and workers during the planning process can make changes easier to implement.

- **Cost** – changing the structure of a firm's workforce will mean incurring costs. Unless sufficient financial resources are available, managers will struggle to put their plans into action.
- **Corporate image** – the general public's view of a business can be enhanced by workforce planning that can then create new jobs. However, large-scale redundancies resulting from relocation are more likely to damage a firm's corporate image, leading to a possible loss of sales.

The value of workforce plans

Effective workforce planning will help to maintain or improve business performance in the short, medium and long term by:

- Recognising the time required to implement policies – for example, recruiting the right employees can take a long time. If managers do not allow for this, resulting staff shortages can result in missed deadlines or poor service, leading to customer dissatisfaction.
- Encouraging HR managers to adopt a coordinated approach – working together with colleagues from other functional areas, such as marketing, operations and finance should help to ensure that corporate objectives are met.

However, the value of workforce planning can be reduced by:

- The quality of the information upon which decisions are based – inaccurate forecasts based on poorly conducted research will reduce the effectiveness of any workforce plan that is put together.
- The impact of unforeseen events – regardless of the level of research or the experience of HR managers, a workforce plan can become irrelevant overnight as a result of the effects of a natural disaster, such as a hurricane or earthquake, a terrorist attack or a severe recession.

Themes for evaluation

Having the right number of workers with the right skills at the right time is essential for effective operations. This is the aim of workforce planning, so the process should benefit any business in any circumstances. The effectiveness of any workforce plan in practice, however, depends on how well managers can forecast demand for and supply of labour, and their ability to formulate policies that meet HR requirements.

Exam insight

Identify what, if any, workforce planning is carried out by the business in the case study. An absence of planning in the past could explain current problems, while a failure to plan now could limit the success of any proposed corporate strategy. Be ready to also question the effectiveness of any workforce planning that may have taken place. The 2008/09 'Credit Crunch' showed that no one can reliably forecast the economy. Therefore all processes that involve forecasting (such as workforce planning) require a humble, reflective approach.

Key terms

Recruitment – identifying the need for new employees, defining the job and the kind of person needed to do it, attracting suitable candidates and selecting the most appropriate.

Redundancy – when a job role is no longer needed to be carried out so that employees holding the job are no longer required.

Workforce planning – comparing future workforce needs to current employee numbers and skills, and formulating plans to deal with resulting issues.

Test yourself (30 marks)

1 Explain the key components of a workforce plan. (3)
2 Jot down two important benefits of workforce planning to each of the following businesses:
   a) Primark, thinking of opening its first shop in India in a year's time.
   b) Barclays Bank, planning to open 200 mini-banks in small towns throughout Britain.
   c) Waterstone's, planning to close half its book shops, switching some staff to work on an expanded online bookstore. (6)
3 Describe one internal influence and one external influence on a firm's workforce planning. (4)
4 Analyse two issues that a firm should consider when implementing a new workforce plan involving staff redundancies. (7)
5 Evaluate the view that workforce planning is of little value for a newly-established firm in a market subject to constant change? (10)

Introduction

You were introduced to the concept of 'organisational structures' during your AS Business Studies course. It refers to the way in which a business is designed to carry out its activities. A firm's internal structure can be illustrated by drawing up a diagram, known as an organisational chart. This will highlight a number of features, including:

- the job roles of individual employees within the business, e.g. directors, managers, and supervisors
- which employees are responsible for (and accountable to) whom
- the routes by which communication flows within the business – both vertically and horizontally.

The organisational structure chosen by a business will impact on its costs, employee relationships and motivation levels and its ability to respond to changes in the market in which it operates.

Types of organisational structure

Common types of organisational structures include:

- **Functional structures** – organising employees into departments representing the main functional areas, such as marketing, production, human resources and finance. Employees have clearly-defined roles and responsibilities within each department, although the authority to make key decisions will be retained by senior management. There are likely to be many levels within the hierarchy and managers will have relatively narrow spans of control.
- **Matrix structures** – putting together teams of employees from different departments to work on specific tasks or projects. The teams are created on a temporary basis until the project is completed and are made up of individuals with specialist skills or relevant experience in a particular area, but with different levels of seniority.
- **Entrepreneurial structures** – having a small number of key employees at the heart of the business. These key figures – often the owners of smaller firms – have strong, perhaps charismatic personalities, in-depth knowledge of the market and other skills that are seen as essential to the firm's success. They have a great deal of power and control decision-making. This tends to produce a relatively flat structure, with few levels of hierarchy. See the table on the next page.

Factors influencing choice

- **The size of the business** – many businesses begin with a relatively simple entrepreneurial structure, built around the owner or owners. As the business grows, the number of decisions and the degree of management expertise required may lead to the adoption of a more complex structure with many layers.
- **The nature of the firm's products and market** – a firm operating in a rapidly changing market might choose to adopt either a matrix or an entrepreneurial structure for increased flexibility. A large, multi-product business may adopt a functional structure with departments of experts in marketing, finance, human resources, etc.
- **Employees' skills and attitudes** – low-skilled or poorly-motivated employees may need a structure with many layers and relatively narrow spans of control. Firms employing highly-skilled and highly-motivated staff, however, may find it beneficial to adopt a matrix structure.
- **Organisational culture** – staff may be used to showing considerable respect to employees in relatively senior positions, leading to a more formal, functional structure.

Adapting organisational structures

Businesses change their operational structures regularly. This will often be in response to changing market conditions, such as increased competition or falling customer demand. The methods used include:

- **Increasing the degree of centralisation** – giving more authority and power over decision-making to senior managers, rather than delegating power further down the hierarchy. This may be appropriate in firms where consistent policies are required, or where customers expect identical standards whenever and wherever products are used. It also means that decisions can be made and implemented quickly. However, decisions may prove to be mistakes, as they may not take account of different customer needs, and will have been made by managers with little, if any, direct contact with the market.
- **Increasing the degree of decentralization** – delegating more authority and decision-making to managers further down the hierarchy, or in branches

Structure	Key advantages	Key disadvantages
Functional	• The duties and responsibilities of individual job roles are clearly defined. • Chains of command are evident.	• Vertical and horizontal communication can be slow and of poor quality. • The business is likely to be relatively slow to respond to changes within the market.
Matrix	• Focuses on individual project needs, creating greater flexibility. • Increased motivation from greater variety and opportunities to lead projects for relatively junior staff.	• Possible conflicts between project and departmental managers over the control of team members. • Inability of senior managers to have an overview of the firm's activities, leading to a loss of coordination.
Entrepreneurial	• Centralised power can mean rapid decision-making. • Relatively flat structures mean that decision-makers are close to (and more aware of) the market.	• The business will be vulnerable to the loss of key employees. • As the business grows, key employees may become over-burdened, affecting the quality of decisions.

or divisions away from their head office. Managers can use their knowledge of local conditions to adapt the goods or services provided to meet customer needs more effectively. It also means that senior managers can focus on developing longer-term corporate strategy. However, junior staff must have the skills and attitudes to manage resources effectively, while working to achieve the firm's corporate objectives.

● **Delayering** – taking one or more layers from an organisation's hierarchy. Often the layers that are removed are made up of staff from middle management. A flatter internal structure is created, speeding up communication, bringing senior managers closer to shop-floor workers and allowing them to respond more quickly to customers' needs. It can raise motivation levels by giving relatively junior employees greater responsibility. Getting rid of relatively expensive employees through redundancy can also reduce overheads significantly over time. However, losing the experience of these middle managers can be damaging in the long term, while the effectiveness of remaining managers may be reduced by greatly increased workloads.

A* insight

Top candidates tend to read every piece of text with a degree of scepticism. A manager says: 'I'm a great believer in delegation and decentralisation'. Really? Is there any evidence to support this, or may it simply be a self-serving claim? According to every company's website, staff are respected and developed. Yet strikes happen – usually when trust between management and staff has broken down. So it is right to be sceptical about whether managers really do what they say.

Themes for evaluation

You may be expected to assess the effectiveness of the firm's current structure. You may also need to suggest and evaluate possible ways that it could be improved. Actions such as delayering that may reduce costs in the short term may be less appropriate in maintaining competitiveness in the longer term.

Key terms

Entrepreneurial structure – where a business is organised around a small number of key players, who take most, if not all, of the key decisions affecting the way the business is run.

Formal structure – the traditional approach of organising employees into departments representing the main functional areas, such as marketing, production, etc.

Matrix structure – where employees from different departments and different levels of seniority are put into temporary teams to work on specific tasks or projects.

Test yourself (25 marks)

1 Explain two factors that could influence a firm's choice of organisational structure. (5)
2 Briefly explain what is meant by a matrix structure. (3)
3 Examine two problems that a growing business could face when attempting to switch from an entrepreneurial structure to a functional structure. (6)
4 Identify one advantage and one disadvantage for a firm of increasing the level of decentralization. (2)
5 Analyse the key benefits and drawbacks for a major UK bank from delayering to attempt to improve competitiveness during an economic recession. (9)

Unit 21 Flexibility and insecurity

Introduction – the need for a flexible approach

A flexible firm is one that is willing and able to adapt its operations easily in response to changing circumstances. The need for a more flexible approach has arisen for a number of reasons, including:

- demands for more customised products, more closely tailored to individual customers' needs
- frequent and often rapid changes within the marketplace resulting from increasing levels of competition
- pressures to reduce costs brought about by competition from overseas firms.

Some firms have adopted lean production techniques in order to become more flexible. This approach implies the use of machinery than can be re-programmed quickly to carry out a range of tasks. It also relies on the creation of a multi-skilled workforce that is willing and able to adapt to the firm's changing requirements.

The business need for more flexibility has had benefits for staff who wanted to move away from full-time, permanent employment, such as parents with young children. Yet it has also meant less job security for some staff, as they have been pushed from secure full-time work to short-term contracts.

Achieving greater workforce flexibility

There are a number of ways in which workforce flexibility can be improved:

- **Functional flexibility** – where employees are multi-skilled and able to carry out a variety of tasks, rather than specialising in one particular job or area. This makes it easier for workers to be kept fully occupied, as they can be switched from task to task, in response to a firm's operational requirements. It also helps to reduce the disruption to production caused by workers being absent or leaving. Achieving functional flexibility requires an investment in workforce training to broaden the range of skills.
- **Numerical flexibility** – using temporary contracts and agency staff, as well as subcontracting or outsourcing certain operations. Increased numerical flexibility can ensure that a business has sufficient capacity to respond to increases in customer demand, without having to bear the cost

of employing workers if there is a temporary sales decline. However, these benefits may be offset by lower productivity resulting from using 'temps' who are less familiar with the way the business operates and also less loyal to it.

- **Time flexibility** – moving away from employing workers for a nine-to-five working day and a 38-hour working week. Some of the increasingly common methods of varying working patterns include the use of part-time work, job-sharing, annualised and zero-hours contracts and flexi-time. A key benefit of introducing greater time flexibility is that firms are able to tailor their operations more effectively to customer needs, increasing the level of convenience offered. Providing employees with more flexible working arrangements can also help to improve recruitment and retention. Homeworking is another type of flexible working arrangement, where employees are based at home for the majority of their working time, with IT links to the firm's main office, via the use of laptops, mobile phones, etc. This approach can help to make significant reductions to a firm's overheads, as the space needed to accommodate staff is much less. However, it may have a negative impact on teamworking as the homeworker may start to feel 'out of the (communication) loop'.

A model of the flexible firm

In an attempt to increase their degree of flexibility, firms may categorise workers as being either 'in the core' or 'on the periphery'.

- **Core workers** – these are workers who possess knowledge and skills and carry out tasks that are central to the firm's operations, making them difficult to replace. They are usually made up of full-time employees on permanent contracts who usually enjoy a great deal of job security. They would be expected to be highly motivated and committed to the achievement of the firm's corporate objectives.
- **Peripheral workers** – these are workers who carry out tasks that support the firm's operations. Although these tasks are necessary, they may require more general skills that are not specific to the firm. Alternatively, they may be highly specialist workers whose skills are not required on a constant basis. These workers are likely to be employed on a part-time or temporary basis, so that they can be replaced, or their numbers changed, relatively

quickly, creating flexibility. The jobs of such workers are, therefore, much less secure.

A* insight

The extent to which any individual business will benefit from the adoption of a more flexible workforce will depend on the circumstances – both internal and external – that the business faces. Top candidates will think about the circumstances of the business identified in the case: Apple would not want temporary staff working on the next iPhone – they want 100% loyal, 100% committed full-timers. Perhaps a supermarket chain would be less worried. Try to establish whether the business is faced with constant changes in market conditions, in which case labour flexibility may be essential.

Handy's Shamrock Organisation

According to Professor Charles Handy, the workforce of a modern firm actually consists of three elements or parts. The model, known as 'The Shamrock Organisation' consists of:

- the core workers – made up of qualified and highly-skilled managers, technicians and other professionals
- the contractual fringe – external individuals, agencies and firms to whom certain operations are outsourced
- the peripheral workforce – made up of temporary and part-time workers.

Insecurity

Increasing the degree of workforce flexibility may, in some circumstances, help a firm to be more responsive to market changes and lead to a reduction in labour costs, boosting efficiency and increasing the ability to compete.

However, one of the greatest drawbacks to creating a workforce with a small core of workers, relative to the periphery, is a potential loss of workforce loyalty and commitment to the firm. The job insecurity experienced by those employed on temporary contracts may lead to much lower levels of motivation than would be the case if workers were employed on a more permanent basis. Maslow's theory identified that insecurity could undermine higher order needs such as self-esteem and self-actualisation; are managers who push for labour flexibility aware of the psychological issues?

Application

Telecommunications giant BT is one of a number of organisations responding to the recession by attempting to increase the flexibility of its workforce of 100,000 employees. The company has piloted a number of schemes, including sabbaticals on reduced pay, flexi-time and part-time contracts. It has also created a term-time contract for employees with children, revising salaries so that they can be spread over the year, allowing staff to continue to receive regular monthly payments.

Source: www.guardian.co.uk

Themes for evaluation

Increasing workforce flexibility can lead to a reduction in costs and an increased ability to respond to changing customer demands. It can also create new challenges for employees, offering opportunities to learn new skills and develop new career paths. However, firms will need to weigh up the impact of these benefits against the potential costs of lower levels of staff loyalty and higher levels of labour turnover that could result.

Key terms

Annualised-hours-contract – where a firm agrees to employ workers for a certain number of hours per year, but can use these as it chooses, rather than having the same number each week.

Flexible workforce – an approach to workforce planning that depends less on the employment of full-time, permanent workers, relying more heavily on the use of part-time and temporary staff, as well as methods such as outsourcing (see below).

Outsourcing – where a firm finds another business to carry out part of its operations, in order to cut costs or to achieve a better level of service.

Subcontracting – where another business is used to carry out part of a firm's operations (see outsourcing).

Zero-hours contract – where a firm hires workers but on the condition that they will only be paid if they are used.

Test yourself (20 marks)

1. Explain the difference between numerical and functional flexibility. (2)
2. Describe two benefits for a firm of increasing the degree of time flexibility within its workforce. (4)
3. State one possible benefit and one possible drawback of outsourcing for a firm. (2)
4. Examine the possible consequences for a mobile phone operator of increasing the number of its sales staff who work from home. (6)
5. Analyse two possible implications of adopting more flexible working practices on the competitiveness of a major UK bank. (6)

Introduction

The relationship between employees and the management of the firm that employs them is a key factor influencing performance. Good relationships can help to achieve a competitive edge and ensure that change is implemented smoothly. Bad relationships can lead to reduced productivity, poor quality and increasing costs. Occasional disagreements between management and staff are inevitable, but good relationships should ensure that they are resolved quickly and effectively.

Managing communications

Communication involves the transfer of information between individuals or groups. Effective internal communication (i.e., within a business) is essential in order to:

- provide accurate, up-to-date and easily accessible information to improve decision-making
- coordinate different areas of the business, ensuring that employees are working towards the same goals
- clarify the roles and tasks that individual or teams of employees should be carrying out
- provide feedback on performance so that it can be repeated or improved.

For any of the above points to happen, communication must be effective. This means that the message has to reach the receiver and be understood in the manner intended by the sender. There are a number of factors that can act as barriers to effective communication:

- **The size and structure of the business** – large firms tend to have many management layers, making vertical communication difficult and slow. The volume of information will also be greater, increasing the risks of communication overload.
- **The leadership style of management** – autocratic managers do not seek the views and opinions of their subordinates, or set up systems to allow two-way communication.
- **The attitudes of employees** – conflict and mistrust between employees and their managers may mean that messages are misinterpreted or ignored. Good news is more likely to be received with scepticism, whereas bad news may be over-exaggerated.
- **Language or cultural issues** – many modern businesses operate across a number of countries and employ staff of different nationalities, using different languages. The use of jargon, gestures and the subtleties of non-verbal communication can also lead to misunderstanding.

In order to make communication as effective as possible, managers need to:

- **Train all employees to improve communication skills** – all employees should understand the importance of communicating clearly, of avoiding unnecessary communication in order to prevent overloading and of choosing appropriate media for communication.
- **Encourage the development of suitable management styles** – talking to, rather than talking at, employees can motivate them, encourage ideas for new products or more effective working practices and allow problems to be identified.
- **Review organisational structures** – flatter structures reduce the time taken for messages to pass up and down an organisation. Greater use of delegation and empowerment can also lead to more effective communication by involving more employees in decision-making.

Methods of representation

Managers may choose to consult with workers over issues involving pay and working conditions. Doing this via employees' representatives is likely to be quicker than consulting each employee individually. Managers may also recognise the potential benefits of encouraging employees to participate in decision-making. Methods of employee participation include:

- **Works councils** – this is a committee of employer and employee representatives, set up to discuss company-wide issues such as training and investment.
- **Staff associations** – organisations within individual (usually large) businesses, made up of representatives who are elected by the workforce.
- **Employee cooperatives** – businesses where all employees are part-owners, giving everyone a right to participate in decision-making.
- **Trades unions** – independent organisations representing the interests of workers across one or more industries or sectors. Workers have greater power by acting together when negotiating with management (known as collective bargaining) than by dealing with them individually (individual bargaining). Traditionally, unions aimed to improve members' pay and working conditions, and take responsibility for organising industrial action in situations of dispute. Even more important today,

is the provision of legal advice and support, e.g. for staff who feel they are being discriminated against. Although trade union membership is much lower today than in the past, unions still have more than seven million members, making them Britain's biggest membership organisations.

Avoiding and resolving disputes

Industrial disputes result from disagreements between management and employees over the conditions under which they are employed. If the dispute cannot be resolved, it may lead to industrial action. There are a number of types of industrial action (see below).

Example	Explanation
Overtime ban	Where employees refuse to carry out work beyond their contracted hours, reducing workforce flexibility.
Work to rule	Where employees carry out no more than the minimum requirements stated in their contracts – again, reducing flexibility.
Go slow	Where employees carry out their duties as slowly as possible without breaking their contracts, reducing productivity levels.
Strike	Where workers withdraw their labour completely for a length of time.

There are a number of steps that a firm can take in order to try to avoid industrial action. These include:

- **Increasing trade union involvement in decision-making** – frequent consultation early on in the decision-making process creates an opportunity to obtain workers' views and build confidence, reducing the risk of disputes.
- **Single union agreements** – where a firm recognises only one union for the purposes of collective bargaining, reducing the chances of disagreements between different unions and the time taken to reach an agreement.
- **No-strike agreements** – where workers and their union representatives agree not to take strike action for an agreed period of time in return for improved pay and conditions.

If disputing parties cannot reach a compromise, one or both sides may turn to the Advisory Conciliation and Arbitration Service (Acas). Acas is a government-funded, independent organisation that provides an impartial service aimed at preventing or resolving industrial disputes:

- **Conciliation** – where an independent party attempts to keep the disputing sides talking, in order to sort out differences and reach agreement. The conciliator remains neutral and does not pass any judgments.
- **Arbitration** – where an independent party considers the arguments of both sides involved in a dispute, before making a decision as to the correct outcome. This decision may be binding, where the sides must accept the decision, or non-binding, where they do not.

Themes for evaluation

There is a strong and positive link between the quality of employer/employee relations and the performance of a business. Evaluation may be based on judgements about the most likely causes of poor relations or the most appropriate methods to improve them for the case study business.

Exam insight

Resist the temptation to write answers that focus on describing the communication media or the methods of employee representation used within the case study business. The examiner will expect a detailed analysis of the benefits or drawbacks of current systems, with reasoned arguments for how to resolve any problems.

Key terms

Arbitration – where an independent party attempts to resolve an industrial dispute by considering the arguments of both sides involved in a dispute, before making a decision as to the correct outcome.

Conciliation – where an independent party attempts to resolve an industrial dispute by keeping the disputing sides talking, in order to sort out differences and reach agreement.

Trade union – an independent organisation set up to protect and improve conditions for their members within the workplace.

Test yourself (25 marks)

1   Explain two reasons why effective internal communications are important for a business. (4)
2   Outline two possible causes of poor communication between managers and workers within a rapidly expanding business. (4)
3   Examine two benefits for a firm of increasing the level of employee representation. (6)
4   Explain the difference between conciliation and arbitration. (2)
5   Assess the view that the long-term success of a business is determined by the quality of its employer/employee relations. (9)

A2 People – an overview

By this stage of your A level Business Studies course you will be expected to be able to take a strategic view of human resources management, rather than focus your answers on individual areas. A major issue is whether HR managers are able to do the same. All HR managers spend time on day-to-day issues concerning recruitment, training, appraisal and dismissal. Not all have the opportunity to think strategically about future workforce requirements and ensure that the business continues to function smoothly. Such strategy should be an integral part of the firm's overall corporate planning if it is to achieve its long-term objectives. But in many companies, the HR professionals have no voice at the key decision-making meetings.

Planning ahead

Adapting the workforce to meet changing needs cannot be done overnight – recruiting, training and even dismissing staff takes time, and the consequences of making hasty decisions can be very costly. Obviously, no firm can be 100% sure of what its future HR needs will be, given that all businesses operate in environments that are subject to frequent change. However, successful planning can help to reduce the risks of being unprepared when changes do take place.

The value of effective human resources management

It would be easy to believe from the wealth of research conducted on areas such as motivation and empowerment, that all modern managers approach human resources management in an enlightened way, recognising the potential of workers to go well beyond simply 'doing their jobs'. It would also be tempting to conclude that the key to increased productivity for any business is simply to listen to employees and hand over decision-making to them! In practice, however, businesses often struggle to manage their human resources successfully. Many managers continue to adopt a hard HRM approach, seeing their staff as simply another resource to be directed and controlled, while many workers continue to carry out dull and unfulfilling jobs.

Getting the right balance

Good HR management is difficult to achieve. It requires maintaining a steady balance between meeting the different needs of employees and meeting the objectives of the business itself, both of which are subject to regular change. Creating and maintaining a highly-motivated and appropriately skilled workforce is also likely to be expensive, but can hold the key to competitive advantage and long-term success. When the economy stops growing, firms often downsize and delayer to cut costs but then suffer from the loss of experienced employees when the economy starts to move forward again.

A* insight

Examiners like to see breadth of understanding and an integrated approach to the subject. Yet they hate to think that they are giving high marks to a student whose subject knowledge is weak. So it is important to 'prove' your functional knowledge – in this case, about managing people – before going on to discuss HR in relation to the business as a whole.

Test yourself (50 marks)

1 Identify one advantage and one disadvantage for a growing business of creating a specialist human resources department to manage workforce issues. (2)

2 Outline two possible human resource objectives for a car manufacturer during a recession. (2)

3 Briefly explain the difference between hard HRM and soft HRM. (3)

4 Identify two factors that are likely to influence the decision to adopt a hard or a soft approach to managing human resources. (2)

5 Identify the main components of a workforce plan. (3)

6 Analyse one possible benefit for a business of carrying out workforce planning. (3)

7 Describe one internal and one external influence on a firm's workforce planning. (3)

8 Briefly examine one key issue that a firm might face when introducing a workforce plan involving major changes to its organisational structure. (2)

9 Outline one advantage and one disadvantage for a firm that has adopted a functional structure. (2)

10 Describe the key features of a matrix structure. (3)

11 Examine one problem faced by a small firm with an entrepreneurial structure as it starts to grow. (3)

12 Give two reasons why a business might decide to change its organisational structure. (2)

13 Outline one possible benefit and one possible drawback of decentralisation for a chain of fast food restaurants operating on a national basis. (3)

14 Give one reason why a business might seek to introduce more flexible working practices. (2)

15 State two ways in which an online retailer could create a greater level of time flexibility within its customer services department. (3)

16 Briefly explain the difference between core workers and peripheral workers. (2)

17 Give two benefits resulting from effective communication within a business. (2)

18 Explain two possible ways of dealing with ineffective communication within a business. (3)

19 Examine one method that a firm with a poor record of industrial relations could use to reduce the level of industrial action taken by its workforce. (3)

20 Briefly explain the difference between conciliation and arbitration. (2)

Case study: Managing people at LV=

Liverpool Victoria (LV=) is the largest friendly society in the UK with more than 2.5 million customers and members and managing around £8.2 billion of assets. It offers a wide range of financial services products, including savings and investment plans, different types of insurance and life cover. As a mutual organisation, it has no external shareholders and operates on the basis of 'one member, one vote', using profits to provide better returns and higher levels of service to its customers. LV= employs over 4,000 workers in 15 locations across the country, including London, Birmingham, Bristol, Exeter, Glasgow, Leeds and Manchester. One of its key human resource objectives is to maintain a workforce of highly talented, customer-focused employees, with in-depth product knowledge and the ability to make customers feel special. Early in 2009, the company launched a range of leadership development courses for staff. According to David Smith, HR director at LV=, ' … it's good to have an injection of fresh talent externally but you've got to have an internal pipeline.'

In 2006, LV= revealed expansion plans aimed at becoming one of the UK's five largest providers of general insurance by 2011. The plan would involve investing £150 million and create up to 500 jobs. In the same year, the insurer signed an outsourcing deal with an Indian firm, 3i Infotech, to handle a number of its business processes. However, in 2008, LV= announced its decision to bring its HR function back in-house. New IT systems have allowed the business to manage its own recruitment processes, including job advertising, candidate screening and selection, more effectively and led to savings of around £3 million in the first year.

Questions (40 marks)

1 Describe two possible human resource objectives that LV= might have. (5 marks)

2 Analyse the key benefits of workforce planning for LV=. (10 marks)

3 Examine the impact on LV= of its decision to bring its HR function back in-house after outsourcing it for a number of years. (10 marks)

4 To what extent would a business like LV= benefit from having a decentralised internal structure? (15 marks)

5 Advanced operations management

Unit 24 Key AS issues in operations management

Introduction

Effective operations lie at the heart of successful business. You need to take a strategic approach to this area at A2 but, to do this, you need a thorough understanding of the operational topics covered at AS. This is confirmed by the AQA A2 specification, which states:

'This section considers operational objectives and strategies that a business can use to achieve success in its particular market. It builds on the AS Operations materials.'

This also means, wherever possible, you can and should use AS operations concepts and theories to answer questions on both A2 exam papers. The key AS operations topics to revisit are:

- Making operational decisions.
- Developing effective operations through quality.
- Developing effective operations through customer service.
- Working with suppliers.
- Using technology in operations.

Making operational decisions

In order to operate effectively, operations managers must plan, organise and coordinate available resources to produce products efficiently and effectively. Setting operational targets helps to monitor how efficiently this is being done. Operational targets usually include:

a) **Controlling unit costs** – the level of unit costs affects profitability, and is particularly important to firms competing on the basis of price.

b) **Managing capacity utilisation** – operating at close to full capacity utilisation reduces unit costs and increases efficiency. If a significant level of excess or spare capacity exists, managers may need to take steps to reduce it. Alternatively, matching output to demand may require capacity to be increased. In this case, managers must decide whether the increase in demand is likely to be permanent or temporary, perhaps as a result of receiving a non-standard order.

Quality

Quality is a difficult term to define. For some businesses, quality is about durability and reliability – for others, it is about a strong image or brand. Whatever the interpretation, there are many potential benefits for firms who succeed in achieving and maintaining high standards of quality. These include higher sales, greater customer loyalty and increased price flexibility.

Traditionally, firms attempted to control quality by employing specialist employees to inspect output and reject any low-grade items. However, the costs involved in not 'getting it right first time' have led some firms to switch from quality control to quality assurance, where employees are given the responsibility for checking their own work. Total Quality Management (TQM) moves beyond being a system for quality assurance; it is more of a business culture, in which all employees within an organisation take pride in providing high-quality products and services.

Customer service

The ability to compete successfully is determined, to a large extent, by a firm's ability to offer consistently high levels of customer service. Surpassing customer expectations creates opportunities for charging higher prices, and minimises the level of resources used up dealing with customer complaints. Delivering high standards of customer service requires regular market research to find out customer needs and opinions (both of which are subject to change) and having the correct systems in place to meet quality targets.

Exam Insight

At A2, you will not be asked any questions that relate directly to any of the AS concepts outlined in this chapter. Nevertheless, top students are those who can easily bring business theory into their answers; the more that it is at your fingertips the easier it is to build convincing arguments within your answers.

Working with suppliers

During your AS course, you looked at the vital role played by a firm's suppliers in managing operations effectively. Good suppliers are not necessarily those that charge the lowest prices, although the cost of supplies affects price flexibility and profits. Suppliers are also chosen on the basis of quality, reliability and flexibility. Some businesses, including Waitrose and the Co-op, recognise the value of developing strong and long-lasting relationships with suppliers. Many other firms adopt a more aggressive approach, threatening to withdraw custom unless they get lower prices and extended credit terms.

Using technology in operations

You have looked at the various ways technology is used by firms to increase productive efficiency, assist design and improve communications. The extent to which any individual business benefits from more technology depends on a number of factors. Technology is often expensive to introduce and although it can generate significant cost savings over the long term, the firm still needs to have access to the finance required. The impact of introducing technology to the workforce should also be considered – extensive retraining in some cases, redundancy in others. In either case, resistance to change should be anticipated, and strategies for dealing with it developed.

Key terms

Capacity – the maximum amount of output that a business can produce.

Capacity utilisation – measures the extent to which a firm's maximum capacity is actually being used and is calculated using the formula (Actual output/Full capacity output) x 100%.

Quality assurance – where quality standards are achieved by giving workers responsibility for checking their own work.

Quality control – where resources are used to inspect output at the end of the production process.

Total Quality Management (TQM) – an approach that encourages all the employees in a business to take responsibility for quality and adopt a 'right first time' approach.

Unit costs – the cost, on average, of making one item of production, calculated by dividing total costs by the number of units produced.

Test yourself (50 marks)

1 Identify two possible operational targets that a firm might have.
2 Explain how unit costs are calculated.
3 Explain what is meant by capacity utilisation.
4 Outline two possible causes of spare capacity.
5 Identify one advantage and one disadvantage for a firm of having 70% capacity utilisation.
6 Describe two methods that a firm could use to reduce spare capacity.
7 Explain the difference between production and productivity.
8 Outline one possible benefit and one possible drawback for a firm of subcontracting part of its production process.
9 Identify two ways in which a business can deliver quality to its customers.
10 Explain the difference between quality control and quality assurance.
11 Outline three key features of Total Quality Management.
12 Examine two implications for a firm attempting to improve its quality standards.
13 Identify two methods that British Airways could use to improve customer service.
14 Analyse two benefits for a firm of improved customer services.
15 State three ways that a retailer such as Marks and Spencer could monitor levels of customer service.
16 Describe two benefits for a business of having good relationships with suppliers.
17 State three factors that could influence the choice of supplier for a new business.
18 Identify two ways that technology could be used by a manufacturer to control stock effectively.
19 Identify two ways that technology could be used to improve communications within a large organisation.
20 Outline two issues that a business should consider before increasing the level of technology used in its operations.

Unit 25 Understanding operational objectives

Introduction

Operational objectives are specific and detailed production targets that are set by a business. All firms attempt to produce goods or services that are fit for purpose, and delivered quickly and on time within pre-determined cost limits. A degree of flexibility is also required so that operations can be adapted easily in response to changes in demand. These objectives need to be fully in line with other functional objectives, such as marketing, human resources and finance, if a firm is to compete successfully in the marketplace.

Key operational objectives

Firms set objectives that relate to:
- **Cost** – controlling costs is a major concern for all businesses. Cost is a major determinant of the price that can be charged and the profit that can be made. The greater the level of efficiency, the lower a firm's costs will be, increasing its ability to compete against rivals and generating more profit for shareholders and investment.
- **Volume** – matching the level of production to demand requires decisions to be made and resources committed based on estimates of future sales. Doing this accurately is essential to avoid missed sales opportunities and disappointed customers without having to bear the cost of holding and even wasting large quantities of stock.
- **Quality** – getting things 'right first time' is important both within an organisation and when dealing with customers. Production time and costs can be significantly reduced by ensuring that quality standards are met. Consistently meeting or even beating customer expectations can give a business a major competitive edge. Customer satisfaction is not just about providing products that are fit for purpose but also about ensuring that they are ready when customers want them, creating a sense of dependability.
- **Time** – the length of time spent on production has a direct effect not only on a firm's costs but also on the availability of products to sell and generate revenue. Being the first producer to get brand new products into the marketplace means opportunities for charging higher prices and developing valuable relationships with customers.

- **Flexibility** – firms need to be able to vary their volume of production quickly in response to fluctuations in demand. If they can also produce a standard range of products that can be easily adapted, they can meet customer needs more precisely. This generates higher levels of customer satisfaction, but the business still benefits from high production volumes, keeping costs down. This flexible approach is a form of lean production.

The importance of innovation

Innovation involves putting newly-invented ideas into commercially successful products and processes. Innovation occurs in two ways:
- **Product innovation** – when a firm develops new goods or services. This is important if it is to continue to keep its customers interested and keep ahead of the competition.
- **Process innovation** – when a firm comes up with new ways of producing goods or delivering services. This also leads to improved competitiveness by reducing costs and increasing the quality and speed of production.

The impact of environmental objectives on operations

A firm's decision to adopt a more environmentally-friendly approach may impact on operations in one or more of the following ways:
- More efficient machinery and production systems may be needed – creating a need for finance for investment.
- Suppliers may need to be changed to those able to provide materials from replenishable or recycled sources – it may take time to build up a relationship with new suppliers that are prepared to be flexible and offer trade discounts or generous credit terms.
- Employees may need retraining – in order to learn to use new machinery and cut down on waste.

Influences on operational objectives

The purpose of setting objectives for any functional areas within a business is to help achieve its long-term goals. This means that the precise nature of a firm's operational objectives is determined by its corporate objectives. Other key influences include:

- **The nature of the product** – a reputation for high quality can support a firm's marketing efforts, so needs to be considered when new products are being developed.
- **The level of demand** – this will determine production volumes and so needs to be accurately estimated.
- **The availability of resources** – the quantity and quality of employees, machinery, supplies and other resources used in the production process determines a firm's own production volumes and costs, as well as the level of quality and degree of flexibility it can offer.
- **The behaviour of competitors** – the degree of competition will affect how much a firm can sell and, therefore, needs to produce. Firms operating in fiercely competitive markets face intense pressures to keep costs as low as possible, unless they can attract sales on the basis of high quality.

Application

Sainsbury's environmental objectives

Respect for the environment is one of Sainsbury's five key commitments. The supermarket has set itself targets relating to reducing its use of packaging, energy and waste. In August 2008, it opened a new flagship green store in Dartmouth, Devon. The outlet has already achieved a reduction in energy and CO_2 emissions of over 50%. More than 80% of the energy-saving functions used at Dartmouth have been implemented in the company's other new stores.

Source: Sainsbury's website

Themes for evaluation

There are many factors that could influence a firm's choice of operational objectives and its chances of achieving them. You may be required to assess which factor will be most influential, out of a number of possibilities. You may also be asked to consider the possible consequences for a business of achieving – or not achieving – the operational objectives that have been set.

Key terms

Efficiency – the degree to which a firm uses its resources effectively, often measured by calculating output per worker (known as labour productivity).

Innovation – turning a newly-invented idea into a commercially successful product or production process.

Lean production – an approach to operations that aims to reduce waste levels as much as possible, using techniques such as just-in-time and flexible specialisation.

Operational objectives – specific and detailed targets that are set by a business in relation to production.

Test yourself (30 marks)

1. Using examples, explain what is meant by an operational objective. (3)
2. Briefly explain why businesses set operational objectives. (2)
3. Analyse two reasons why keeping costs as low as possible is particularly important for firms operating in fiercely competitive markets. (6)
4. Describe two benefits of increased operational flexibility for a manufacturing firm. (4)
5. Examine one reason why high standards of quality can give a firm a competitive edge over rivals. (3)
6. Outline three factors that are likely to influence the objectives set by a business. (6)
7. Briefly explain two ways in which innovation can benefit a business. (4)
8. Explain one way in which the decision to set environmental objectives might affect a firm's operations. (2)

Unit 26 Operational strategies: economies and diseconomies; optimum resource mix

Economies of scale

Economies of scale occur when unit or average costs fall as a result of an increase in a firm's level of output. Lower unit costs create opportunities to charge lower prices, making a firm more competitive. They can also lead to higher profit margins, increasing the funds available for investment or allowing for higher dividends for shareholders, making it easier to attract finance in the future. Key economies of scale include:

- **Purchasing economies** – suppliers may be prepared to offer discounts for bulk-buying, as large orders help them to shift stock more quickly, reducing warehousing costs and improving cash flow.
- **Technical economies** – using machinery can lead to greater efficiency in production but small firms may not have the necessary finance for investment. Short production runs mean that machinery would be idle for much of the time. However, large scale production means the fixed costs of purchasing machinery would be spread over higher levels of output, reducing the capital costs per unit.
- **Specialisation** – in a small firm, one person – usually the owner – has to make decisions about marketing, finance, operations and human resources, but may lack the knowledge to do this effectively. Larger firms generate enough work to justify employing specialist teams in these different functional areas, leading to improved performance.

Diseconomies of scale

Diseconomies of scale occur when unit costs increase as a result of an increase in the level of output. The main reasons for this include:

- **Poor motivation** – workers within large organisations sometimes end up feeling like 'small cogs in a big wheel', with little influence over the production process or their working lives. This leads to feelings of powerlessness and alienation, increased lateness and absenteeism, which, in turn, may lead to a reduction in productivity and, unless wages are directly linked to output per worker, increased unit costs.
- **Poor communication** – direct, face-to-face communication becomes more difficult as the workforce grows. The speed of communication slows down as the length of time taken for messages to be sent and received increases. It also becomes more difficult to check that messages have been understood or even received. If the effectiveness of communication decreases, workers may not understand what they are meant to be doing – mistakes will be made, leading to an increase in the amount of waste.
- **Poor coordination** – as a firm expands, it acquires more resources, takes on more workers and sets up new areas or branches. Controlling all of these resources so that operations continue to run smoothly becomes an increasingly complex business. Workers may need monitoring to ensure they remain on task, adding to costs.

Diseconomies are not inevitable, nor do they occur automatically once a certain size is reached. However, growth does affect the way a business operates. If growth is well-planned and not too rapid, strategies can be developed to allow the firm to adapt and avoid problems in the first place, or deal with the diseconomies that do occur. These strategies include:

- **Creating a more suitable internal structure** – delayering could increase the speed of communication and the amount of delegation that occurs, improving motivation. Decentralisation could also help to tackle coordination by giving managers in different areas of the business greater authority and control.
- **Increasing the level of worker empowerment** – giving employees the power to plan how their work is done can overcome motivation problems by increasing their input into the decision-making process and helping them to see more clearly how their individual efforts impact on business performance.
- **Creating new communication systems** – initiatives such as quality circles and works councils can create opportunities for meaningful, two-way communication. Technology can also be used to increase the effectiveness of communication in many situations, if used appropriately.
- **Training managers and employees** – knowing how to delegate is a valuable skill, but both managers and subordinates need to be trained for the process to be successful. New communications systems can work, but only if staff are able and willing to use them appropriately.

A* insight

The term 'economies of scale' tends to fudge together two quite separate factors. Top students will be able to see the differences between them. The first is the unarguable benefit that comes from increasing a firm's capacity utilisation. If higher sales mean higher capacity utilisation, average costs will certainly fall. The second issue is when firms increase their capacity, e.g. move to a much bigger factory. Here, the benefits of scale may apply, but there are far more likely to be significant diseconomies of scale as well. Really, the term economies of scale should apply only to the second of these factors.

The optimum resource mix

When planning the production of goods or services, managers must decide whether production should be capital intensive or labour intensive. Over the years, the degree of capital intensity in many areas of industry has increased. Machines work faster and for longer, are more reliable, do jobs that are repetitive and dull and involve working unsociable hours. Technological advances have made machines more flexible and able to perform complex tasks. However, increasing the degree of capital intensity may meet with resistance from workers, who may be reluctant to retrain and fearful of redundancy. Change needs to be carefully managed, therefore, to prevent employer/employee relations deteriorating. There are also still some areas such as sales, customer care, product design and management where human knowledge, experience and creativity continue to be an essential resource.

The resource mix chosen will therefore vary from business to business and is likely to be influenced by the following:

- **The nature of the product and processes used** – standardised goods aimed at mass markets are more likely to be produced using capital intensive methods than products where a great deal of design variation is required.
- **The cost and availability of resources** – for example, capital intensity in manufacturing has increased to reduce unit costs and compete against firms in low-wage Asian countries.
- **The availability of finance** – although it can generate significant cost savings in the long term, capital equipment is expensive. Unless a firm can raise sufficient investment funds, it may be forced to continue to use less efficient, labour-intensive methods.

Application

Google

Despite having locations around the world and employing thousands of staff speaking many languages, Google's senior management team are determined to maintain the firm's 'small company feel' and unconventional approach in order to foster creativity and innovation. Workspaces remain littered with pool and ping pong tables, lava lamps and video games. In an attempt to prevent continuing growth from stifling communication, the company now also runs regular meetings. Employees are encouraged to share new product ideas with Google co-founders, Larry Page and Sergey Brin, and chief executive, Eric Schmidt.

Sources: Google website, The Economist

Themes for evaluation

You may be required to:
- assess the extent to which an expanding business might benefit from economies of scale or suffer from diseconomies
- make judgements on whether a capital intensive or labour intensive system of production would be most appropriate for a business.

Key terms

Capital intensive production – when a relatively high level of machinery is used in the production process, relative to other inputs.

Labour intensive production – when a relatively high level of labour is used in the production process, relative to other inputs.

Scale of production – the level of output produced by a firm.

Test yourself (15 marks)

1 Explain what is meant by the term 'economies of scale'. (2)
2 Briefly explain two types of economies of scale. (3)
3 Explain what is meant by the term 'diseconomies of scale'. (2)
4 Explain one benefit and one drawback for a firm of adopting more capital intensive production processes. (4)
5 Explain two influences on the choice between labour intensive and capital intensive production. (4)

Unit 27 Research and development and innovation

Introduction

Innovation involves taking a newly-invented idea and turning it into a commercial success. Product innovation leads to brand new goods and services, allowing the firm concerned to enjoy the benefits of being the first in the market. New products, such as the iPhone, focus on needs that customers did not even know existed, generating high levels of customer loyalty if these needs, once awakened, are satisfied successfully. Firms also benefit from developing new methods of production that can increase efficiency, reducing costs so that lower prices can be charged. This type of innovation, known as process innovation, allows a business to stay ahead of competitors and maintain or increase market share.

A key part of the innovation process is research and development (R&D). This involves using scientific and technical processes to develop new products and processes, or improve existing ones. Large organisations, particularly in sectors such as pharmaceuticals, aerospace and electronics, have the resources to fund facilities dedicated to R&D. For example, in 2006, confectionery manufacturer Cadbury opened a new $40 million research facility in New Jersey to support its efforts in challenging rival Wrigley's position as leader of the global chewing gum market.

The innovative firm

Successful innovation is not just the responsibility of highly talented and highly paid scientists, locked away working in R&D departments, but requires the involvement and support of all of the key functional areas of a business, including:

- **Operations** – new ideas need to be produced at the volume, quality and cost levels required to become a commercial success. It is the responsibility of the production department to develop the systems and to design or acquire the machinery and train employees to manufacture new products as efficiently as possible.
- **Human resources** – in many businesses, all employees are seen as potential sources of new ideas and are encouraged to contribute their ideas via quality circles, *kaizen* groups and suggestion schemes. Some organisations create specialist research teams containing employees from areas

such as finance and marketing, as well as R&D scientists, all of whom can give their expert opinions on how to create successful products.

- **Finance** – designing or improving products and processes requires long-term investment and is relatively high risk. Resources are used up on projects that may take years to generate a significant income stream and, in most cases, will not succeed in even reaching the market.
- **Marketing** – the role played by market research in identifying customer needs and opinions is crucial to success. In addition, although a great 'product' lies at the heart of a successful marketing mix, the other ingredients – price, promotion and place – also need to be effective.

Application

It is possible to overdo product innovation. Kit Kat was Britain's number one chocolate product until new owners Nestlé decided to boost its sales further. Over a period of two years Nestlé brought out Strawberry, Yogurt and Lemon, Christmas Pudding and many other innovative flavours. The result was that Kit Kat sales fell by 16%. Customers ended up confused about the Kit Kat brand itself.

Protecting ideas

Preventing rivals from copying newly-invented ideas gives a business the chance to generate as much revenue as possible, once products are launched. This allows it to recoup development costs and provide funds for future innovation. There are a number of forms that protection can take:

- **Patents** – taking out a patent gives a firm the right to be the sole producer or user of a new invention for up to twenty years. Patents can also be sold or licensed to other firms. The patent holder has the right to sue any other firms it suspects of copying patented ideas, but this can be expensive, time-consuming and difficult to prove. Patents only apply to original technical ideas such as the dual cyclone that Dyson used to replace the vacuum cleaner.
- **Trademarks** – logos, symbols and words such as brand names are all used to distinguish products within the market. They can also be protected from imitation by being registered at the Patent Office.

- **Copyright** – the work produced by writers, artists and musicians is automatically protected under the law, so does not need to be registered. However, it is still the copyright holder's responsibility to take action against any offenders.

Innovation – benefits and risks

Successful innovation can improve business performance in a number of ways. Key benefits include:

- **Greater price flexibility** – being the only supplier in the market means that a price skimming strategy can be adopted, maximising the revenue generated when the new product is launched. Price can then be reduced as competitors begin to appear, helping to retain market share.
- **Market power** – operating as the sole supplier of a product gives a firm a great deal of control over price and supply. The length of time this can go on for depends on how quickly rivals respond with copycat products.
- **Improved reputation** – an established track record of successful innovation can be a valuable marketing tool. New product launches by companies such as Sony and Apple attract a great deal of media attention, raising consumer awareness and encouraging sales.

However, innovation requires managers to commit resources now in the hope of generating long-term returns that are difficult to quantify. Common problems include:

- **Obtaining the necessary funds** – banks are likely to be reluctant to lend money to finance high-risk projects, while shareholders may only be interested in using profits to generate quick returns.
- **Reaction of competitors** – it may not be possible to recoup the funds invested in new product development if competitors are able to quickly develop their own versions, especially if they are able to benefit from initial teething problems by producing better alternatives.

Application

It took 15 years and over 5,000 prototypes before James Dyson launched his DCO1 Dual Cyclone vacuum cleaner in the UK in 1995. Within two years, it had become the number one seller. In 1999, he was forced by his rival, Hoover, to go to court in order to sue for patent infringement. The manufacture of vacuum cleaners was transferred to Malaysia in 2002 but the company's headquarters in Malmesbury, Wiltshire, continues to act as the base for its Research and Development Centre. Over a third of the site's

1,200 employees are the scientists and engineers responsible for new product and technological development.

Source: www.dyson.co.uk

Themes for evaluation

Assessing the value of innovation may well involve comparing the short-term costs to the potential benefits. The process involves risk and requires long-term commitment, so any firm looking for quick and safe returns is unlikely to set innovation as a key objective.

Exam insight

One of the toughest of all business decisions comes when sales are going well for a brand that may have become a cash cow. Should you bring out a new product that will take sales mainly from your existing, cash-rich brand? Innovate? Or wait? Apple quickly swept its launch of iPhone aside for a better model, whereas other firms wait to take as much profit as possible from one brand before launching the next. Decisions such as this are exactly what is meant by the term 'strategic thinking'.

Key terms

Innovation – successfully bringing a new idea to the workplace or marketplace.
Invention – the creation of a new product or process.
Research and development – using scientific and technical processes to develop new products and processes, or improve existing ones.

Test yourself (20 marks)

1 Explain the difference between invention and innovation. (4)
2 Explain the difference between product innovation and process innovation. (4)
3 Analyse the implications of adopting a strategy of innovation for the main functional areas of a business. (8)
4 Identify two ways in which a firm could benefit from becoming more innovative. (2)
5 State two factors that might discourage a business from becoming more innovative. (2)

Unit 28 Industrial and international location

Introduction

The factors that influence a firm's choice of site to base its operations include cost and proximity to suppliers, customers and appropriately skilled staff. New businesses often lack the resources to afford a location that meets all of their needs, often compromising on the basis of what is affordable. The main reasons why an established business may rethink its original choice of location are:

- **As a result of a decision to expand operations** – operating on a larger scale may require larger facilities, if maximum capacity at the existing site has been reached. Expansion may also involve operating on a number of sites – either nationally or internationally.
- **As a result of relocating operations to a better site** – potential new sites need to be assessed by comparing potential benefits to the costs involved. For example, will existing staff be prepared to move, or will they have to be made redundant and new employees recruited?

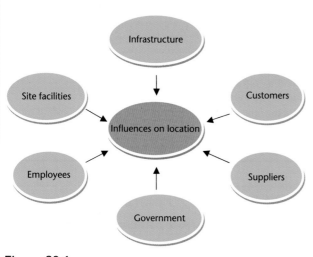

Figure 28.1

Quantitative methods

Access to accurate data can improve the chances of getting the choice of location right. The quantitative decision-making techniques that are commonly used include:

- **Investment appraisal** – techniques such as payback and average rate of return can be applied to assess the financial viability of a project. Alternatively, investment appraisal can help a firm choose between two or more proposed locations.

- **Break-even analysis** – location costs, such as rent charges, business rates and interest on loans for land purchase, act as fixed costs. If these costs increase, more has to be produced and sold in order to maintain profits. However, a more convenient location that improves the firm's image can increase sales or mean that higher prices can be charged.

Formula reminder

Average rate of return (ARR) = (Average annual return/Initial outlay) × 100%

Break-even point = Fixed costs/Contribution per unit

Qualitative influences

Location decisions are rarely made purely on the basis of finance. The way an area looks, emotional attachments or the opportunity to enjoy a better quality of life may also be influential, although their importance is more difficult to quantify. A geographical concentration of firms from the same industry can create external economies of scale, such as easier access to suppliers and skilled workers. Often, a location's association with a particular industry continues to attract firms long after the original reasons for moving there have gone. This is known as **industrial inertia**.

International location

A multinational organisation is a business with production facilities in different countries. A firm may choose to develop an international dimension in order to:

- **Open up new markets** – targeting foreign markets can maintain sales growth for expanding businesses operating in slow-growth or saturated domestic markets. It may also offer some protection against the effects of recession at home.
- **Benefit from cheaper labour** – paying lower wages for both unskilled and skilled workers in other countries can result in significant cost reductions. Recent EU enlargements have stimulated UK manufacturers to move to the Czech Republic, Hungary and Poland.

- **Benefit from lower land costs** – cheaper land, lower taxes and more lenient legislation in areas such as health and safety may also have the effect of reducing fixed costs.
- **Reduce transport costs** – as markets become more globalised, an increasing number of UK firms are finding that the majority of their customers and suppliers are not based in the domestic market at all. Relocation may, therefore, bring about considerable gains by reducing the cost and time spent on transporting goods around.
- **Reduce the effects of exchange rate fluctuations** – importing and exporting is an uncertain business. An increase in the value of sterling, for example, could damage export markets as goods produced here become more expensive. Relocating so that production takes place in the countries where goods will eventually be sold offers some protection against exchange rate changes.
- **Overcome trade barriers** – governments and trading blocs such as the European Union (EU) use a range of measures, including tariffs, quotas and non-tariff barriers, to try and protect domestic markets from foreign competition. If these measures are effective, the only way that foreign firms can gain access is to set up production facilities within the market itself.

The practice of **offshoring** has become increasingly common among UK firms in recent years. The activities are either carried out in facilities owned by the firm, or completely outsourced to another. Activities that are routinely 'offshored' include HR functions, call centres and IT, although there is a growing trend towards higher-value roles, particularly in financial services and research and development.

Risks of international location

There are a number of potential problems that should be considered by any business before making the decision to locate in another country. The main risks are:

- **Impact on public image** – UK redundancies and accusations of worker exploitation in low-wage economies is likely to attract media attention, generating negative publicity that could damage sales, especially if the firm concerned claims to behave ethically.
- **Cultural differences** – ensuring that communication remains effective in a multi-site organisation with a multilingual workforce spread over a number of time zones is a big challenge.
- **The degree of economic and political stability** – developing economies and democracies are subject to frequent and rapid changes that can damage a firm's performance and even threaten its survival.

Themes for evaluation

Faced with a number of locations, it is impossible to know whether a firm has made the right choice after the decision has been made. Judgements have to be made on the basis of the criteria that are most important at the time – for example, a business trying to project an upmarket image may be prepared to accept higher rental costs to secure the 'right' site.

A* insight

Location decisions incorporate two of the broadest and most powerful forms of business analysis: quantitative versus qualitative factors and trade-offs between profits and ethics. The latter is especially fertile ground for A* answers. Relocating a business almost always means that some long-standing staff will lose their jobs. Is this ever acceptable morally? Perhaps it is, on the grounds that the firm's long-term survival depends upon change. But it is right to be alert to occasions when profitable firms have no moral right to cast aside the staff who have built the business to where it is today.

Key terms

External economies of scale – cost advantages enjoyed by a business resulting from the growth of the industry in which it is located.

Industrial inertia – when businesses continue to locate in an area even after the original benefits of doing so have gone.

Multinational – a business with productive facilities in more than one country.

Offshoring – relocating one or more business processes from one country to another.

Test yourself (15 marks)

1. Outline two reasons why a business might decide to relocate. (2)
2. Identify three factors that might influence a firm's decision to relocate. (3)
3. State two quantitative methods that could assist a business in making its relocation decision. (2)
4. Suggest two reasons why a UK manufacturer might consider relocating overseas. (2)
5. Explain what is meant by the term 'offshoring'. (2)
6. Outline two reasons why UK firms should be cautious about relocating operations overseas. (4)

Introduction – what it means to be lean

Lean production is an approach to operations that aims to minimise all forms of waste, in terms of materials, energy, time and human effort. Waste increases the costs of production. Materials have to be reworked or thrown away and replaced, and workers have to be paid to repeat production, creating delays that may lead to missed sales opportunities. Increasing levels of international competition, particularly from low-cost economies such as China and India, has meant that firms in many industries have had to cut prices in order to survive. Many firms have been forced to look for new ways of increasing efficiency in order to protect their profits.

Reducing waste through time-based management

Cutting the time to get goods or services to customers can give a firm a competitive edge, especially where customers place a high value on speed and convenience. Reducing the time it takes to design and develop new products in response to changing customer tastes is also important. Firms may use **simultaneous engineering**, which brings together all of the different staff involved in a new product's design to work on the project at the same time, rather than one after another.

Reducing waste using critical path analysis

Critical path analysis (CPA) is a planning technique used to organise all the different activities required to complete a complex project in the shortest possible time. Once the project has been broken down into separate tasks or activities, CPA identifies:
- the time required to complete each activity (the duration)
- the correct sequence for the activities
- which activities can take place simultaneously
- which activities cannot run over without delaying the project overall (critical activities).

Once this has been done, a critical path (or network) diagram can be drawn. This shows how all of the activities (drawn as straight lines) either follow or run alongside each other. The start or end of an activity is indicated by a circle, known as a node. The diagram must begin and end with a single node, denoting the start and the finish of the project.

Once the diagram has been set out correctly, the next step is to calculate the earliest start times (EST) and latest finish times (LFT) of each of the activities:
- EST of any of the activities flowing out of a node is given in the top right-hand section. The figure tells us the earliest time that the activity can begin. It is calculated by adding together the EST from the previous node and the preceding activity with the longest duration. The EST of each activity must be completed first by moving from the left to the right of the diagram.
- LFT of any of the activities flowing into a node is given in the bottom right-hand section. The figure tells us the latest time that a preceding activity must be finished, to avoid delaying the whole project. LFTs are calculated by starting at the end of the diagram and moving left. The duration of the longest activity is subtracted from the LFT to the right of it to give the LFT for the next node on the left.

The EST and the LFT in the final node must be equal, as this gives the overall length of the project. The longest path through from start to end is the **critical path**.

Benefits	Drawbacks
• It reduces the risk of anything being overlooked that could endanger overall success. • Reducing the time taken to get products to customers can create a competitive advantage. • Identifying exactly when resources are needed allows firms to reduce costs by, for example, ordering stocks just-in-time. • Managers can concentrate on completing critical activities, ensuring customer deadlines are met.	• Estimates of activity duration may be inaccurate, particularly for a brand new product or market, reducing the accuracy of CPA results. • Successful implementation depends on managers' skills, as well as the availability of resources such as finance and skilled labour. • Managers can become rigid and inflexible, even if more efficient alternatives are thought up.

Table 29.1 Benefits and drawbacks of using critical path analysis

A* insight

Lean production is not a 'magic bullet', to be shot into the body of a struggling business. It is one element in a business culture based on flexibility, waste-minimisation and continuous improvement. This means two key things: that the management of operations and the management of the staff (HRM) must work in harmony; and – even more important – that it would always be wrong to suggest 'switching to lean production' as a short-term fix for a problem. Successfully introducing lean production might take three to five years to be really effective. That's not to say it isn't worth trying; as General Motors found before its US government bail-out in 2009.

Other techniques used in lean production

- **Just-in-time production (JIT)** – involves producing to order, rather than holding large quantities of finished goods in stock, and bringing in raw materials and components from suppliers just as they are needed by the production department. Holding stocks of finished goods allows a business to respond quickly to unexpected orders, while stocks of raw materials act as a buffer if supplies are interrupted. However, stocks are expensive to hold – they need to be warehoused safely and insured against damage or theft. They occupy space that could be used for production and tie up working capital. They may deteriorate, become obsolete or become unfashionable, increasing wastage levels. Reducing the need to hold stocks can, therefore, reduce costs significantly. However, for JIT to be effective, a business has to rely on suppliers to deliver high-quality, defect-free goods when they are needed.
- **Cell production** – this involves separating the production process into a series of self-contained stages, rather than having a continuous flow. Employees are organised into teams, and each team is responsible for a specific production stage. Within the team, workers are encouraged to carry out a range of different tasks, making them multi-skilled and more flexible. Teamwork and greater responsibility can increase worker motivation, leading to higher productivity, better quality and lower waste levels.

Application – Starbucks

The effects of recession and increased competition appear to have been the main reasons behind the decision by Starbucks to adopt lean production. The initiative began in 2008 and involved a 'lean team'

of ten staff going into restaurants across the US, observing working practices of coffee house *baristas* and looking for ways to improve efficiency and speed up delivery. In one store, moving whipped cream, chocolate and caramel drizzle toppings closer to where drinks were served to customers shaved eight seconds off the 45-second process.

Themes for evaluation

Every student knows the problem of trying to become more efficient (at revision, perhaps?). It is easy to claim to parents that hours of work are being done. And it is easy to kid yourself. Much the same is true of lean production. Nearly every manufacturing business claims to have a lean operation. Evaluation can often be shown by unpicking what the business says and what it does. What is the evidence for its leanness? Words are not evidence, only deeds.

Key terms

Cell production – where the production process is broken down into different stages, carried out by teams of workers.
Critical path – the activities in a network that must be completed in the shortest possible time so that the duration of a project can be minimised.
Just-in-time production – an approach of manufacturing that sets out to minimise the cost of holding stock.

Test yourself (20 marks)

1 Briefly explain what is meant by 'lean production'. (2)
2 Outline two benefits of implementing time-based management. (4)
3 Explain what is meant by 'critical path analysis'. (2)
4 Analyse one benefit and one drawback of critical path analysis (4)
5 Identify two ways in which just-in-time production can reduce costs. (2)
6 Explain why supplier relationships are important for firms using JIT production. (3)
7 Examine one benefit for a firm that may result from introducing cell production. (3)

Unit 30 Continuous improvement

The *kaizen* approach

Kaizen is the Japanese term for continuous improvement. The approach is based upon the view that firms can always find ways of doing better. It believes that a firm's greatest resource is its employees. It encourages all workers to examine their performance and their working environment more or less constantly, looking for small-scale improvements in productivity or quality. These changes can be put forward by using *kaizen* group or quality circle meetings. Small changes tend to be more acceptable and, therefore, easier to introduce than major changes but, over time, the overall impact of these changes on a firm's performance can be significant.

In order for *kaizen* to work, a special culture needs to be created, which is accepted and adopted by all employees within a business. The main features of the *kaizen* culture include:

- **One employee, two jobs** – employees must be prepared to carry out the tasks assigned to them and also be prepared to scrutinise their roles, looking for ways to carry them out more effectively. By carrying out jobs day in, day out, workers become experts within their area and are, according to *kaizen*, more able to spot problems and solutions than managers.
- **Empowerment** – this involves giving workers the power to decide how their work should be carried out, and the authority to make changes that they feel are necessary to improve performance. Motivation may also be increased by giving employees greater control over their working lives.
- **Teamworking** – being part of a team (or cell) encourages workers to support each other and share ideas. The expertise of individual workers within the team increases over time as they carry out all of the tasks within their section and acquire more skills. Their broad understanding makes it easier for them to generate ideas for improvement.

Potential difficulties of implementing *kaizen*

There are a number of potential obstacles that could prevent a *kaizen* approach from being implemented successfully. These obstacles include:

- **Increased costs** – introducing *kaizen* requires both workers and managers to be trained, in order to understand the process and acquire the necessary skills, leading to increased costs and lost output. Managers may struggle to justify this, particularly if the resulting benefits are hard to quantify.
- **Employee resistance** – managers may resist the empowerment of shop-floor workers because they resent the weakening of their authority. Workers may also object to changes – they may not trust managers to implement suggestions and resent the additional responsibility and increase in workload.

The limitations of *kaizen*

Although *kaizen* can be beneficial in helping to improve business performance in areas such as productivity and quality, it is not appropriate in all situations. The main limitations of the approach include:

- **Diminishing returns** – initially, the volume of ideas generated is likely to be high, as employees may be enthusiastic about participating in a new initiative and solutions to relatively straightforward problems are put forward. However, as time goes by, it may be difficult to maintain enthusiasm and the pace of improvement may slow down.
- **The need for radical solutions** – a series of small changes occurring gradually over time may not be appropriate for all firms. Some will require major changes to be implemented quickly, rather than a gradual evolution, in order to survive. Business process re-engineering (BPR) requires a firm to completely rethink its current operations and redesign them from scratch.

Figure 30.1 The value of *kaizen*

Application

The global economic slowdown has led to a significant increase in the number of firms in India interested in adopting *kaizen* techniques in order to cut costs and maintain profits. According to Jayant Murthy, one of the directors of the *Kaizen* Institute of India, 'two years ago it was difficult to convince a CEO of driving improvements in the organisation,' but the Institute has experienced a 25% increase in enquiries from Indian firms during 2009.

Source: Business Standard

Themes for evaluation

Adopting a *kaizen* approach can bring many benefits to a business but its implementation can also be highly disruptive. You may need to assess whether any possible problems can be avoided, or resolved quickly, and make judgements as to whether these short-term costs will be outweighed by the long-term benefits of increased productivity and improved quality.

A* insight

Kaizen is a cultural issue rather than a strategy. This means it is hard to establish, and may take years, even decades, to become a real success. Yet the savage economic downturn of 2008/2009 showed the need for firms to be able to take drastic actions when necessary. Toyota struggled to establish a major restructuring, perhaps because of its *kaizen* approach. Strong exam candidates appreciate that there are never any magic solutions to business problems.

Key terms

Business culture – the prevailing attitudes, management style and general behaviour of the employees within a specific business.

Business process re-engineering – a radical approach to change, where a firm is completely redesigned in order to improve performance.

Kaizen – the culture of continuous improvement.

Empowerment – giving workers greater control over their working lives and the power to decide what to do and how to do it.

Quality circle – a group that meets regularly to identify quality problems and discuss possible solutions.

Teamworking – when production is organised into large units of work carried out by groups of multi-skilled workers, rather than using flow production, where workers complete the same task repeatedly.

Test yourself (20 marks)

1 Briefly explain what the term '*kaizen*' means. (2)
2 Explain why an employee has to be prepared to carry out two jobs for *kaizen* to be successful. (3)
3 Explain why worker empowerment is important to the *kaizen* approach. (2)
4 Explain why effective teamworking is important for *kaizen* to be successfully implemented. (2)
5 Analyse one reason why *kaizen* can increase motivation levels within the workforce. (3)
6 Give one reason why a business introducing *kaizen* might experience an increase in costs in the short term. (2)
7 Examine two reasons why a firm's attempts to introduce *kaizen* might meet with resistance from employees. (4)
8 Identify two limitations of the *kaizen* approach. (2)

Continuous improvement

During your A2 course, you will have studied a number of new operations concepts to add to those introduced at AS level. Naturally, you will be expected to demonstrate an in-depth understanding of all of these elements, but the examiner will want more. In order to award high marks, he or she expects you to move beyond this to see the importance of operational decisions to the overall strategy of the business. Any changes to a firm's operations will affect its other functional areas, so make sure you think through the implications of any recommendations for marketing, human resources and finance.

Operations are central to any business, regardless of its size or the sector in which it operates. The ability to produce appealing and reliable products as efficiently as possible holds the key to continued business success.

Achieving and maintaining effective operations can only become more important as competition becomes fiercer. Future enlargements of the European Union – perhaps taking in countries such as Turkey or more central and eastern European states – and the further growth of the BRIC economies (Brazil, Russia, India and China) will place even more pressure on UK firms to find ways of keeping costs as low as possible.

Test yourself (65 marks)

1 Briefly explain how a firm's operational objectives are linked to its overall corporate objectives. (3)
2 What is meant by the term 'efficiency'? (2)
3 Examine two ways in which a business can benefit from increasing the efficiency of its operations. (4)
4 Give two possible environmental targets that a large retailer, such as Sainsbury's, might choose to set. (2)
5 Explain what the phrase 'fit for purpose' means in relation to quality. (2)

6 Describe two ways that customers might assess the quality of the following products: a) a Sony Vaio laptop; b) a Domino's pizza. (4)
7 What is meant by the term 'economies of scale'? (2)
8 Identify and briefly explain two types of economies of scale. (4)
9 Explain what is meant by diseconomies of scale. (2)
10 Analyse two benefits for a firm of becoming more capital intensive. (4)
11 Outline two reasons why a business might continue to use labour-intensive production processes. (2)
12 Briefly explain the difference between invention and innovation. (3)
13 Identify one benefit and one drawback for a business of investing heavily in research and development. (2)
14 Give two reasons why an established firm might decide to relocate. (2)
15 Briefly outline two quantitative techniques that might be used as part of the relocation decision. (4)
16 State two qualitative factors that could influence the choice of location. (2)
17 What is meant by the term 'offshoring'? (2)
18 Identify three pieces of information that can be obtained from a network diagram. (4)
19 Explain the purpose of lean production. (2)
20 Outline two ways in which a business can benefit from using time-based management. (2)
21 State one benefit and one drawback of using critical path analysis in planning new projects. (2)
22 Briefly explain what just-in-time production involves. (2)
23 Why are excellent relationships with suppliers necessary for firms using just-in-time production methods? (3)
24 What is meant by the term 'kaizen'? (2)
25 Identify two conditions that would ease the successful implementation of kaizen. (2)

Case Study – Dell Computers

Dell was set up in the United States in 1984 by Michael Dell to produce computers for home and business use. Dell believed that, by selling directly to customers rather than through retailers, consumer needs could be better understood. The company's computers are built to order, taking a basic model and then customising it according to specific customer requirements. This way, customer needs are satisfied more effectively and the company still benefits from high-volume production, keeping unit costs down. Dell supplies the ten largest companies and top five commercial banks in the US, as well as being the main supplier of computers to small and medium businesses for the last ten years. The company employs over 65,000 people globally, with factories in the US, Europe and Asia.

Dell owes its success to the use of lean production techniques. All of the company's manufacturing facilities use the same processes to ensure that quality standards are the same and so that best practice can be identified and implemented. Production is 'pulled' or triggered by customer demand. The process only begins when an order is received and finished goods are dispatched immediately, avoiding the need for warehousing. This also allows the company to keep materials stocks to an absolute minimum, meaning that the components used are as up-to-date as possible. Production is highly capital-intensive and is based around the principle of 'single person build', where whole items are assembled by one worker. Dell also embraces the *kaizen* philosophy of continuous improvement. According to company CEO, Kevin Rollins, 'We want every employee to be responsible for and every pair of eyes to be focused on anything we can do better.'

Dell manages its operations within three geographic areas or regions – the Americas region, the Europe, Middle East and Africa (EMEA) region and the Asia Pacific Japan (APJ) region. All of these regions contain a number of manufacturing and distribution facilities, to minimise the time taken between customer purchase and delivery. Several business centres are also located in each region, where sales and technical support staff are based. According to the company's website, the global nature of its operations generates a number of key benefits, including a better understanding of customer needs, a wider range of employee skills and ideas and access to a greater number of suppliers, helping to increase quality and reduce costs.

The industry in which Dell operates is highly competitive and the company's strong commitment to innovation has undoubtedly helped its performance. It has established innovation facilities in China, India, Singapore and Taiwan, as well as at its headquarters in Austin, Texas. Despite this, in recent years Dell has lost its position as market leader to rival, Hewlett Packard.

In January 2009, Dell announced its decision to relocate its European manufacturing base from Limerick, Ireland to a factory in Lodz, Poland. The move was part of a $3 billion cost-reduction strategy announced in 2008 and meant the loss of 1,900 jobs from the 3,000 strong workforce. Until this point, Dell had been Ireland's biggest exporter, largest technology company and second largest company overall. Switching operations from a high-cost to a relatively low-cost location was also encouraged by a €54 million subsidy from the Polish government. The decision was approved by the EU Commission because of Lodz's unusually low standard of living and high unemployment levels.

Sources: Reuters

Questions (50 marks)

1 Analyse two consequences for Dell resulting from the increase in its scale of operations. (10)
2 Examine the key benefits for Dell from implementing lean production techniques. (10)
3 Discuss the importance of innovation to a company such as Dell. (15)
4 To what extent do you agree with Dell's decision to relocate its European manufacturing base from Ireland to Poland? (15)

6 Advanced external influences

Unit 32 Introduction to external influences

Introduction

External influences are factors that are beyond the control of a business, but that can still affect its performance. The impact can be favourable or unfavourable, depending on the nature of the influence. Firms must take account of the potential impact of external influences on their performance. A business may have to adjust its strategy, perhaps in response to a recession. Companies can make huge mistakes by ignoring changing times. The great economist John Maynard Keynes once said: 'When the facts change, I change my mind. What do you do, sir?'

Types of external influences

Business performance can be affected by a number of external factors, including:

- **Economic factors** – the rate of economic growth, levels of consumer expenditure and changes in unemployment are all likely to have an effect on the level of demand for a firm's products. Basic commodities, such as oil, wheat and copper, act as an input into the production process, so changes in their prices affect business costs. In addition, Government policies that attempt to influence the level of economic activity can also have an impact on business performance.
- **Legal and political factors** – the introduction of new laws and regulations can affect businesses in a number of ways. The creation of the National Minimum Wage in the UK in 1999 increased labour costs for many firms, causing some to rethink their recruitment plans. The ban on smoking in public places, introduced in July 2007, led to a fall in customer numbers in many pubs and clubs, but arguably may have increased sales for off-licences and pizza delivery services as more people chose to stay at home.
- **Technological factors** – changes in technology can create opportunities but also pose threats for business. The development of the Internet has given even the smallest of UK firms the chance to advertise and interact with customers on a global scale. However, it has also increased the choice of products available. For example, the availability of cheap – and often free – music and video downloads has forced a number of music retailers out of business.
- **Demographic factors** – demography looks at changes in the size and structure of the population. For a number of decades, the UK's population has been ageing, with more people living further into old age and fewer babies being born. These changes have boosted demand for a range of products aimed at the elderly, including medical services and residential care. Possibly the most significant (and controversial) demographic change in the UK in the last decade has been the increase in immigration. This occurred as a result of the EU expansion of 2004, which created ten new members, including Poland and the Czech Republic. Workers from these countries migrated to the UK to benefit from its relatively high wage rates, providing a cheap source of labour for UK businesses. This helped keep economic growth high and inflation low for the period 2004–2007.

Dealing with external influences

It has already been noted that individual firms, no matter how big, have no control over external influences. However, this does not mean that they are powerless. They need to be prepared for the unexpected. For example, if a workforce is committed to the business, it will be willing to make short-term sacrifices, as JCB workers did by taking a pay cut in 2008/09.

Other examples include:

- Businesses that have a broadly-based product portfolio can cope more easily with external change, e.g. BMW, with its three main brands: BMW, Mini and Rolls-Royce. In bad times customers might switch from BMW to Mini; in better times it might be Rolls-Royce that enjoys a sales boom.
- Firms that operate in fiercely competitive markets may not be able to prevent new rivals from setting up, but they can look for ways of improving efficiency in order to keep costs low, and maintain excellent standards of service in order to generate customer loyalty.

The ultimate goal for a director of a large organisation is to try to internalise the external objectives, i.e. to bring them within the control of the managers. Strictly speaking this is impossible, yet it does not prevent it being a key objective. It is why major businesses such as British Airways and Virgin Atlantic collude (illegally) to fix prices. And it is why huge multinationals such as Unilever like to be diversified, i.e. to reduce their dependence on any one product, brand or market.

A* insight

Good students can distinguish clearly between internal and external influences, giving effective examples. Top students are able to see that internal and external influences can interact. In 2009 Cadbury was fighting against a takeover approach from the giant US Kraft food business. This external factor coincided with a period when the Cadbury management had been extremely tough in pay negotiations with the workforce. A July 2009 headline read: 'Cadbury workers furious over pay rise offer as company creams off profits'. Staff had been offered a 0.5% annual pay rise while profits rose 24%. It was noticeable during the early stages of Kraft's bid that Cadbury staff did little to defend the company against the US takeover. Internal factors were interacting with external ones.

A* success comes from 'an ability to see complexity where others see simplicity; and to see simplicity where others are floundering.'

Application

Domino's Pizza is one of the few businesses that has benefited from recession, as people prefer home delivery to eating out at restaurants. During the first half of 2009, aggressive advertising and discounts helped the company's sales to grow by 15.4%, with online sales rising by nearly 40% and profits going up by 25%. According to a Domino's spokeswoman, the swine flu virus could also give a boost to its UK sales, mirroring its experience in Mexico where the outbreak of the disease had a positive impact on demand for home deliveries.

Source: www.guardian.co.uk

Themes for evaluation

The extent to which any business is affected by changes in the external environment depends, to some extent, on whether or not it was possible to predict the change. A business that takes its present situation for granted and chooses not to respond to known events, such as changes in employment or consumer law, is highly likely to fail in the long term. Those firms that anticipate and prepare for change have a much greater chance of success. This is likely to be the case even when change is unexpected, as they are likely to have developed a culture that can respond to change more effectively.

Exam insight

External changes do not affect all firms in the same way. For example, the impact of an economic downturn on a retailer such as Marks and Spencer is likely to be largely negative, whereas a discount supermarket like Aldi may actually experience an increase in sales. It is vital therefore, that you are clear about the nature of the business you are dealing with before you begin to consider whether an external change represents an opportunity or a threat.

Key terms

Demographic changes – changes in the size or structure of the population of a country.
External influences – factors that are beyond the control of a business, but that can still affect its performance.

Test yourself (15 marks)

1 Explain what is meant by an external influence. (2)
2 Briefly explain two ways in which a retailer selling electrical goods might be affected by an increase in interest rates in the UK. (4)
3 Identify one firm that would benefit and one firm that would suffer from the UK Government's decision to place a total ban on advertising junk food, explaining how each firm would be affected. (4)
4 Examine one way in which a commercial bank could take advantage of an increase in the number of people using the Internet. (3)
5 Identify two ways in which a supermarket chain could be affected by a significant fall in the number of people under the age of 21 in the UK. (2)

Unit 33 Impact on firms of economic variables

Economic growth

The size of an economy is measured in terms of the value of the goods and services it produces – formally known as gross domestic product (GDP). In order for an economy to grow, it needs to produce more goods and services, compared to previous years. It can do this by acquiring more resources, for example, immigration increases the amount of labour available. Economic growth can also be achieved by using technological innovation to increase the productivity of resources.

Economic growth brings huge benefits:
- If an economy produces more goods and services, there are more products for people to consume, leading to an increase in their standard of living. Your parents may remember China as a country of starvation and bicycles. There was hardly a private car on the road 15 years ago. In 2009 China's car market outstripped that of the US to become the world's biggest. This is the result of 15 years of stunning growth rates averaging 10% a year.
- Economic growth also makes it easier for new, small businesses to set up, and existing ones to expand.

The business cycle

The rate of growth for an economy tends to be uneven. Regular fluctuations in the rate of economic growth over a number of years are referred to as the business or trade cycle. Business cycles are characterised by four stages:
- **Boom** – periods of rapid economic growth. Unemployment is low, with some firms struggling to fill vacancies. Consumers are optimistic, resulting in high levels of consumer spending. Business confidence is also high, with increasing levels of investment for both replacement and expansion projects.
- **Recession** – the term used to describe an economic slowdown, although, technically, it implies two successive quarters of negative growth, i.e., falling output. Unemployment rises and consumer spending starts to fall. The number of business failures increases, reducing confidence and leading to a fall in investment. Inflation begins to fall as firms start cutting prices to maintain sales; this was the position of most of the world's economies in the first half of 2009.
- **Slump** – a period where falling output is particularly lengthy or severe. GDP is strongly

negative and unemployment is high, resulting in even lower levels of demand. Inflation is low and prices may even be falling (known as deflation). Businesses are likely to be very pessimistic about the future, with no plans for investment.
- **Recovery** – when output within the economy begins to grow again. Both consumer and business confidence starts to return, as demand begins to increase. Unemployment eventually begins to fall and firms start to invest in order to expand.

Unemployment

Unemployment is caused by a fall in the demand for labour, relative to its available supply. Rising unemployment occurs during recessions. Firms produce less due to falling demand and, therefore, need fewer workers. This type of unemployment, known as cyclical unemployment, falls as the economy recovers, once firms become more confident and increase production. Structural unemployment results from the decline of an industry within an area. Workers remain unemployed even when the economy is booming because they lack the skills required. The level of unemployment is also influenced by factors affecting the supply of labour, such as migration, and those affecting the demand for labour, including technological innovation.

Rising unemployment can create both advantages and disadvantages for businesses, depending on the circumstances of the individual firm.

Advantages include:
- Recruiting new staff should become easier and the quality of applications should improve, as more people are looking for work.
- Labour turnover may fall, due to the reduced number of job vacancies, reducing the need (and cost) of recruitment and induction training.
- The number of industrial disputes is likely to fall, as workers become more concerned about keeping their jobs.

Disadvantages include:
- Falling incomes lead to a reduction in consumer spending, which could mean that demand for a firm's products is reduced. However, the extent to which a firm is affected depends on the nature of its products and the action it takes to maintain sales.
- A 'de-skilling' of the workforce if unemployment is long-term, as workers lose skills that they once possessed and fail to acquire any new ones. This, in turn, leads to lower productivity and increased training costs when workers are recruited.

The 'macro' economy is complex, especially when you start analyzing the effect of one economic factor on another, e.g. the impact of interest rates on exchange rates. Although A*s come from showing your qualities, this is not a good area for 'showing off'. In business courses examiners are interested in how well you can analyse the impact of economic factors on the business in question. Beware of analysing the impact of economic factors on other economic factors. Understandably, that's economics not business studies!

Inflation

Inflation measures the annual increase in the average level of prices within an economy. As long as incomes increase in line with price rises, households are no worse off. However, inflation causes a number of problems for businesses. These include:

- Inflation can damage profitability if firms cannot pass on increased costs of supplies or machinery to customers. For example, a business may have signed a fixed price contract that takes a long time to complete.
- Inflation can damage competitiveness, both in domestic and overseas markets, if UK prices are rising faster than those in other countries.
- Inflation can damage employer/employee relations if managers resist attempts by workers to protect living standards by increasing wages.

However, inflation can also benefit firms by increasing the value of assets, such as property and machinery, and creating a more impressive balance sheet, which can be used to secure finance. In addition, firms with high levels of existing debt should find it easier to repay it, as a result of rising levels of income and profits.

Exchange rates

An exchange rate is the price of one currency in terms of another, e.g. the value of the pound in terms of dollars or euros. Exchange rate fluctuations cause the price of imports and exports to change, and can have a dramatic effect on profitability.

An appreciation (increase) in the value of the pound has the following implications for UK firms:

- **The price paid by foreign customers for UK exports rises** – this could lead to a fall in demand (depending on the degree of price elasticity). In order to maintain sales, a firm might choose to cut its export prices, but this then leads to a fall in export revenues.

- **The price of imports into the UK falls** – this reduces the costs of production for manufacturers importing raw materials, boosting profits and creating opportunities to reduce the price of finished goods. However, firms competing in the domestic market with products produced overseas face tougher competition.

The affects of a depreciation (fall) in the exchange rate are the reverse of those for an appreciation.

Key terms

Business cycle – regular fluctuations in the rate of growth of an economy over a number of years.
Exchange rates – the price of one currency in terms of another, e.g. £1 = €1.15.
Inflation – a sustained increase in the average level of prices within an economy.
Unemployment – when someone wishes to work but is unable to find a job.

Themes for evaluation

The extent to which any individual firm suffers during a recession or makes the most of a booming economy depends to a large extent on the nature of the business and the ability of its managers to anticipate and respond to changes effectively.

Exam insight

The exam paper is likely to contain a lot of economic data and it is important that you understand it, but avoid writing lengthy descriptions of it all. Instead, focus on analysing the most relevant data – to do this you must have a clear understanding of the business, its operations and its markets.

Test yourself (15 marks)

1 Identify two characteristics of
   a) an economic boom,
   b) an economic slump. (4)
2 State one benefit and one drawback for a firm operating in an economy with high levels of unemployment. (2)
3 Explain two effects on a business of rising inflation in the UK. (3)
4 The value of the pound has just depreciated against the euro – will UK exports to France now be cheaper or more expensive? Justify your answer. (2)
5 Chase Vodka exports 60% of its production to the US. Examine two actions the firm could take in response to an appreciation in the value of the pound against the dollar. (4)

Unit 34 Developments in the world economy: globalisation and development

Globalisation

The term 'globalisation' refers to the increasing trend for markets to become international in nature, sharing the same characteristics and making it easier for businesses to operate on a worldwide scale, rather than concentrating on one country.

Globalisation presents a number of potential benefits for UK businesses:

- **Opportunities for increased sales** – free trade gives firms easier access to foreign markets. This gives firms an opportunity to increase revenues and generate higher profits, if they are able to compete successfully in these markets.
- **Scope for increased economies of scale** – operating on a larger scale can reduce unit costs significantly, spreading the fixed costs such as capital investment and marketing over a much greater level of output, particularly if a business is able to produce and sell a standardised product on a global scale.
- **Access to cheaper resources** – opportunities to locate production in areas where the cost of land, labour and supplies are low can increase the efficiency of business operations.
- **Access to better quality labour** – operating on a global scale also gives firms greater opportunities to find the best qualified or skilled employees, with a better understanding of local markets and customer needs, meaning that products can be designed to match these needs more closely.

However, globalisation also poses a number of potential problems for UK firms, including:

- **Increased competition** – reducing or removing trade barriers makes it easier for foreign firms to compete in the UK. Many of these firms are based in developing countries, where goods can be produced at a lower cost. Most UK manufacturers have found it impossible to compete against cheap imports purely on the grounds of price. Instead, many have attempted to differentiate their products by investing to improve quality and develop strong brands.
- **The threat of takeover** – growth by takeover gives businesses faster access to world markets. Taking control of established foreign firms whose products are already well-known by customers is also likely to involve less risk. Successful UK firms may, therefore, find themselves increasingly vulnerable to takeover by large multinationals.

- **Criticisms of exploitation** – firms that locate or use suppliers based in low-wage economies often attract negative publicity. The extent to which this could damage sales depends on whether customers are prepared to accept this behaviour, in order to continue buying cheap products.

A* insight

The term 'globalisation' implies an assumption that products and trade are becoming increasingly standardised worldwide. In other words the same few multinationals increasingly impose their brands (Coke, Starbucks, BMW, et al) on every country in the world. The risk here is the word 'increasingly'. In the 1920s and 1930s Ford and General Motors pushed their cars on the world. At the beginning of the twenty-first century European Airbus and US Boeing made all the world's large passenger planes. Yes, all of them. But by 2009 China had made its first new plane and Japan was also planning to open its own aircraft factories. In other words, globalisation is nothing new; and it may be that the future will see a wider band of countries competing internationally – not a smaller one. A* candidates must make up their own minds about issues such as this.

Emerging economies

An emerging economy or market is one where average incomes and living standards are currently low, but where economic growth rates are high, implying much higher levels of production and demand in the future. By 2009, a decade of phenomenal growth in manufacturing output had made China the third largest economy in the world, behind the US and Japan. Other key emerging economies include India, Brazil and Russia (who, together with China, are often referred to as the BRIC countries).

Emerging economies offer a number of potential benefits for firms in established markets. These include:

- **Opportunities to sell to new markets** – both China and India have populations of over one billion, many of whom have rapidly growing incomes, creating sales opportunities for a range of consumer goods and services.
- **Access to cheaper labour** – a large population also creates an abundant supply of workers

competing for jobs and prepared to accept low wages, relative to those in established economies.

- **Access to natural resources** – many emerging economies, such as Russia and Brazil, contain vast supplies of valuable natural resources used by industry, including iron ore, tin, copper and oil.

However, operating in emerging markets also poses a number of challenges, in addition to the problems commonly associated with foreign markets, such as exchange rate fluctuations, language and cultural differences:

- Emerging economies tend to be more volatile, more likely to suffer from high rates of inflation and more vulnerable to recession.
- Despite the potential for future high income and demand, current consumption levels are likely to be relatively low, limiting the chances of generating significant profits.
- Poor communications and infrastructure may lead to delays and increase costs.
- Local employees and managers may lack the skills and experience required by large firms.
- Governments may not welcome foreign firms and create obstacles, including import restrictions and high taxes, to protect domestic businesses.

Business strategies for a changing world economy

A business cannot prevent changes from occurring in the world economy, but the nature of its response is likely to determine whether it continues to survive. Possible responses include:

- **Expanding by selling in overseas markets** – this can generate higher revenues and greater economies of scale, reducing costs.
- **Takeovers or merging with other firms** – merging with a competitor can also generate economies of scale, whereas taking over a supplier could reduce materials costs.
- **Moving production to low-cost locations** – lower operating costs can help firms to compete more effectively on the basis of price.
- **Targeting market segments with highly-differentiated products** – selling lower volumes to groups of customers where brand image and quality, rather than low prices, act as a key influence on sales.
- **Reducing the scale of operations** – firms may accept lower sales volumes within existing markets and, therefore, choose to cut productive capacity, to reduce fixed costs and maintain profitability.

Application

UK number one smoothie maker, Innocent, announced its decision to sell a £30 million stake of its business to fizzy drinks multinational, Coca-Cola. At the time, Innocent claimed that the injection of finance would be used to support its further expansion into Europe but would not change the way the company was run or affect its ethical values.

Source: www.guardian.co.uk

Themes for evaluation

You may be required to assess the impact of globalisation for a given business. Alternatively, you could be asked to evaluate the benefits and drawbacks for a firm of adopting a global strategy.

Exam Insight

The impact of and response to changes in the world economy depends on the circumstances faced by an individual business. For example, does the firm have the resources to operate on a global scale? Does it operate in markets that are likely to attract competition from cheaper overseas competitors, and how will consumers react?

Key terms

Economic growth – an increase in the size of an economy, as measured by a rise in the level or value of the goods and services produced.

Emerging economy – an economy or market where average incomes and living standards are currently low, but where economic growth rates are high.

Globalisation – the increasing trend for markets to become international in nature, sharing the same characteristics and making it easier for businesses to operate on a worldwide scale.

Test yourself (15 marks)

1. Briefly explain what the term globalisation means. (2)
2. Examine two opportunities created by increasing globalisation for UK firms. (4)
3. Analyse two possible threats caused by globalisation for UK firms. (4)
4. Identify one benefit and one drawback for UK firms from emerging economies, such as China and India. (2)
5. Examine one strategy that could be used by a UK clothing manufacturer attempting to respond to increased competition from firms based in countries such as China, India and Bangladesh. (3)

Unit 35 Impact of government economic policy

Government economic objectives

Changes in output, the level of employment, the rate of inflation or the value of the exchange rate can have a significant effect on business performance. The Government tries to manage the economy to create the conditions required for businesses to perform as effectively as possible.

Governments may set economic objectives in an attempt to do the following:

- **Encourage steady economic growth** – rising incomes mean consumers have more to spend on the goods and services produced by firms, boosting their profits and creating opportunities for further growth.
- **Maintain low levels of unemployment** – more people in work increases output and income levels, allowing firms to expand.
- **Create price stability** – keeping inflation low helps firms to plan ahead more effectively and makes it easier for them to compete against foreign rivals, both in domestic and overseas markets.
- **Achieve a favourable balance on the current account** – the Government tries to avoid current account deficits (where the total value of imports is greater than that for exports), because they have to be financed by borrowing or asset sales.
- **Achieve a stable exchange rate** – fluctuating exchange rates make it difficult for firms to forecast the cost of imported materials, as well as the revenues that they are likely to earn from exports.

In recent years, governments have tended to prioritise price stability (low inflation) and steady economic growth.

Government economic policies

Macroeconomic policies are designed to create a supportive environment in which firms can operate, by avoiding the extremes of the business cycle. There are a number of different types of policy that the Government can use, including:

Fiscal policy

This involves using government expenditure or taxation (or a combination of both) to influence the level of economic activity. The Government is a major employer and source of demand within the economy. It also makes **transfer payments**, including the state retirement pension, unemployment benefits and family tax credits. A change in government spending on areas such as health, education or the armed forces has a direct impact on the industries linked to them. The government is a huge customer for businesses that supply books, building and construction work, computers and many other things. Government spending accounts for around 40% of all the spending in the UK.

Changes in taxation can affect firms in a number of ways, depending on the type of tax and the nature of the change:

- **Income tax** – the level of income tax determines a household's disposable income and has a direct effect on consumer spending. An increase in income tax may reduce demand for goods and services, although firms producing luxury items are most likely to be affected.
- **Corporation tax** – this is paid by companies and is levied on the profits they make. An increase in corporation tax will, therefore, reduce the level of post-tax profit, leaving firms with less to reinvest.
- **Expenditure taxes** – Value added tax (VAT) is placed on most retail products, making them more expensive. Other indirect taxes include excise duty, which is levied on a range of goods, including alcohol, cigarettes and petrol. A change in either tax will, therefore, affect sales, to an extent that depends on the price elasticity of the product.

'Expansionary fiscal policy' means government expenditure is greater than taxation, creating a budget deficit and causing the overall level of demand within the economy to rise. 'Deflationary fiscal policy' means that tax revenues are greater than the level of government expenditure, resulting in a budget surplus sucking demand out of the economy.

Monetary policy

Monetary policy influences output and demand by adjusting the amount of money circulating in the economy. In theory, monetary policy can involve changes to the interest rate, control of the money supply or exchange rate manipulation. However, since the late 1990s the main policy tool has been the use of interest rates. An increase in interest rates tends to reduce economic activity. People and businesses feel worse off and so they spend less. A reduction in interest rates boosts the economy, helping to pull a country out of recession. However, the impact of interest rate changes depends on the size of the increase or decrease, the initial level and the state of the economy overall.

Effects of an interest rate rise	Implications
Taking out new loans becomes more expensive.	• Investment projects may be postponed or cancelled. • Falling sales of expensive consumer durables and services, such as cars, furniture and foreign holidays (usually financed by credit).
The cost of some types of existing debt rises.	• Highly geared firms with variable rate loans and overdrafts experience a significant rise in fixed costs, reducing profits. • Households with high levels of personal debt suffer from a fall in discretionary income, reducing expenditure.
The value of the exchange rate rises.	• High UK interest rates, relative to other major economies, attract capital inflows, increasing the demand for sterling and pushing up its value. This makes UK exports more expensive in foreign markets and imports into the UK cheaper.

Table 35.1 The effects of a rise in interest rates

Supply-side policies

These policies aim to increase the productive capacity of the economy, creating more output to meet customer demands. They tend to focus on specific sectors of the economy and might include:

- **Actions to increase labour market flexibility** – the Conservative approach to this has been legislation to reduce trade union power. This makes it easier for firms to make workplace changes – and harder for employees to resist these changes.
- **Attempts to increase the quality of education and training** – increasing workers' skills and knowledge can make them more productive.
- **Attempts to increase the incentive to work** – this could involve reducing unemployment and social security payments, tightening benefit entitlement rules or increasing free child care provision.
- **De-regulation** – removing legal barriers to entry into markets can help to make them more competitive and can lead to greater efficiency.

A* insight

Many of the issues in this section of the course are the subject of fierce debate between the major political parties. Top candidates should be aware that Conservative and Labour governments will tend to have different economic objectives and policies. These differences, such as laws governing trade unions, will affect businesses. You need to be aware of the debates involved and of the general attitude of the business community. You do not need, though, to agree with that attitude. The business community may be confusing what is good for them personally (such as scrapping inheritance tax) with what is best for the economy.

Themes for evaluation

You may be asked to comment on the degree to which an individual business might be affected by changes in government macroeconomic policy or to assess the most appropriate response.

Key terms

Fiscal policy – policies that involve the use of government expenditure or taxation (or a combination of both) to influence the level of economic activity.

Monetary policy – policies that use adjustments to the amount of money circulating in the economy to influence the level of economic activity.

Supply-side policy – policies that aim to increase the productive capacity of the economy.

Transfer payments – government spending that takes the tax income from one social group to fund payments (such as the old age pension) to another.

Test yourself (20 marks)

1 Briefly explain why the Government would wish to influence the level of economic activity. (2)
2 State three macroeconomic objectives that the Government could have. (3)
3 Outline two ways in which the Government could implement an expansionary fiscal policy. (4)
4 Examine two ways in which a furniture retailer could benefit from a cut in interest rates. (5)
5 Give two examples of supply-side policies and briefly explain how they can increase the level of output in the economy. (6)

The European Union

The European Union (EU) is a community of countries, including the UK, that form a single market, allowing the free movement of goods, services, people and capital between members. The EU was created by the Maastricht Treaty in 1993, though the European community dates back to 1957. Britain joined in 1973.

The EU has undergone a series of expansions, with current membership standing at 27 countries. The potential benefits of enlargement include:

- **Access to a much larger market** – EU membership means that UK firms operate in a market of over 500 million people. This creates significant sales opportunities and the chance to benefit from increased economies of scale. UK exporters to other EU countries do not have to face trade barriers, such as tariffs or quotas.
- **Free movement of people** – workers from within the community are free to take jobs in any member state, allowing firms to fill vacancies and expand output. The increased supply of workers keeps wage rates down, helping firms to control costs more effectively.
- **Free movement of capital** – firms are able to switch locations more easily to countries where operating costs are lower and there are fewer restrictions on business activity, such as employment and health and safety legislation.

Despite the progress made in removing many of the trade restrictions that previously existed, the EU 'single market' is nevertheless made up of 27 countries. They have many languages, diverse cultures and, despite the creation of the Eurozone (see below), a number of currencies. These differences must be considered by firms when formulating strategy. Some businesses adopt a **pan-European** strategy, e.g. same brand name and advertising throughout Europe. Others, in effect, treat Europe as having 27 niches, each requiring slightly different products and locally produced advertisements.

The single European currency

The euro was introduced as the single European currency on 1st January 1999. Since then, it has been adopted by 16 of the 27 EU members, who collectively make up the Eurozone. The euro is used on a daily basis by over 300 million people. To date, the UK Government has chosen not to adopt the euro and has no immediate plans to do so. Operating outside the Eurozone means that UK firms lose many of the benefits that a single currency creates. Most notably, exchange rate fluctuations between sterling and the euro make it difficult for firms to accurately forecast import costs and export revenues. Adopting the euro would make it easier to compare the prices charged by UK suppliers with those from other EU countries. This price transparency would allow consumers to compare prices more easily, benefiting those UK firms that can produce more efficiently than Eurozone rivals.

Free trade

For more than 50 years, governments around the world have tried to reduce protectionism and increase the level of international trade. Since 1995 this movement has been led by the World Trade Organisation. The WTO. promotes free trade in goods and services by encouraging countries to abolish tariffs and quotas. It also deals with trade disputes that arise. Members must abide by its rulings and trade sanctions can be imposed against those that ignore its decisions. By July 2008, membership of the WTO had risen to 153 countries. China joined in 2001 but Russian membership is still to be agreed.

Despite the benefits of free trade, there are many countries and pressure groups that have criticised the behaviour of the WTO. Some argue, for example, that it does not pay enough attention to the problems faced by developing countries.

The remarkable success of Chinese economic growth began with policies that protected its domestic markets from foreign competition until the businesses were strong enough to cope. The WTO makes it difficult for less developed countries to use import restrictions to provide temporary protection for their **infant industries**. Some, therefore, accuse the WTO of being a 'rich man's club'.

The impact of legislation

UK firms are subject to both UK and EU legislation. The main areas are:

- **Consumer protection legislation** – sets out to make sure that consumers receive fair treatment when buying goods and services from firms. Minimum legal standards ensure that products actually do what they claim, that they are correctly labelled and are safe to use.

- **Health and safety legislation** – aims to give protection to both employees and customers within the workplace. The Health and Safety at Work Act (1974) requires employers to provide a safe working environment for staff and train them to carry out their jobs without risk of injury
- **Employment legislation** – is designed to protect the rights of employees at work. It covers a huge range of issues, including pay and working conditions, dismissal, discrimination, maternity/paternity leave and trade union membership
- **Legislation to protect the environment** – is designed to reduce the negative impact of business on the climate and environment and can affect the materials and production processes used, the disposal of waste and the extent to which products are designed to be recycled at the end of their use.

Legislation acts as a constraint on business activities and, in many cases, leads to significant increases in operating costs. However, breaking the law is likely to lead to prosecution, resulting in heavy fines and compensation payments, as well as the longer term damage to a firm's reputation. Modern consumers are also unlikely to tolerate poor quality products and illegal trading practices, switching their loyalty to firms that operate within the law. Nevertheless, consumers have repeatedly needed protection from the operations of firms in some industries, notably Financial Services i.e. the banks.

Application

In October 2008, the Financial Services Authority (FSA) imposed a record fine on Alliance & Leicester of £7 million for mis-selling Payment Protection Insurance (PPI) to customers. PPI is often sold when people take out mortgages, loans and credit cards to cover repayments if the policyholder is made redundant or unable to work. The FSA enquiry found that, between 2005 and 2007, the bank's sales staff had repeatedly failed to make it clear to customers that the inclusion of PPI was optional when loans had been taken out. They had been trained to pressurise customers who questioned it. According to research carried out by consumer watchdog, *Which?*, only 11% of people with PPI ever make a successful claim.
Source: Which?

Exam insight

Remember that the impact of changes in government policies depend largely on the circumstances in which individual businesses find themselves. For example, a capital intensive business employing highly-skilled staff is less likely to be affected by an increase in the minimum wage than a labour intensive firm with a large workforce on low wages. So, make sure you have a clear understanding of the case study firm and its operations.

Themes for evaluation

Questions are likely to focus on the extent to which an individual firm will be affected by changes in government policies. Alternatively, you could be asked to suggest or assess the strategies adopted by a business in response to any changes that occur.

A* insight

There is a Latin phrase that is worth remembering and using: *caveat emptor*. It means: 'let the buyer beware'. In other words it is always wise to be a bit suspicious when buying something. Therefore no amount of consumer protection legislation should stop you questioning the seller.

Free market thinkers believe that consumers would make better buying decisions if there was no government involvement, i.e. no legislation. Then people would have to judge for themselves, on the principle of *caveat emptor*. In an exam, the ability to raise the language level within an answer can provide a useful edge. But the term *caveat emptor* will prove useful far beyond the exam.

Key terms

Eurozone – a term used to refer to the EU members that have adopted the single European currency.
Free trade – when trade between countries is not restricted by barriers such as tariffs or quotas.
Infant industries – new industries in less developed countries that may not yet have the skills and scale to compete with established international companies.
Pan-European – a business strategy that treats the whole of Europe as a single, standardised market.
Single market – steps taken by the EU to eliminate trade barriers in order to create one home market made up of member states.

Test yourself (15 marks)

1 Examine two benefits for UK firms from the expansion of EU membership. (4)
2 Explain one implication for UK firms of the decision of the UK government to remain outside of the Eurozone. (3)
3 Briefly outline the role of the World Trade Organisation. (2)
4 Identify two ways in which employment legislation affects UK firms. (2)
5 Analyse two benefits for a UK manufacturer from adhering to consumer protection legislation. (4)

Unit 37 How firms respond to potential and actual changes

Introduction

All businesses operate in a dynamic environment so must be able to cope with change if they are to survive and prosper. Firms need to plan for all potential changes that could impact significantly on performance, rather than wait for changes to occur.

Changes to marketing strategy

Possible changes include:
- **Changing the product portfolio** – this could involve modifying existing products, adding new brands or removing those that are not successful. For example, a supermarket's decision to expand into new, overseas markets might require it to use a different store format than the one used at home. A firm will also need to decide when to withdraw support for products that are failing to meet sales targets. But it can be hard to distinguish between a 'dog' and a 'problem child'.
- **Changing image** – company and brand image can influence demand significantly and changing image can attract customers from different segments within the market. Customers can be suspicious and react badly to this type of change, especially when firms attempt to go 'upmarket'. Firms also need to be careful that the launch of cheaper products does not harm existing demand for the luxury brands they produce.

Changes to operational strategy

Possible changes include:
- **Changing existing facilities** – upgrading existing production facilities can increase efficiency, allowing a firm to increase production and reduce unit costs. However, if demand is falling and is unlikely to recover in the long term, the decision may be taken to rationalise operations by closing down facilities. This will reduce fixed costs and help to maintain profits. Such decisions are usually only taken after careful consideration. Worker redundancies can increase costs significantly in the short term. Reducing capacity will also mean a loss of flexibility to respond to unexpected increases in orders.

- **Changing location** – this may be done for a number of reasons. Forecasts of increasing demand may require an increase in capacity. Relocation may also take place in order to reduce operating costs, or to be closer to suppliers and new markets.
- **Subcontracting** – contracting out orders to other firms allows businesses to increase their capacity, without having to invest in new plant and equipment or expand their workforce. Some firms sub-contract all of their production to other firms in order to increase operational flexibility. However, subcontracting reduces the level of control that a business has over how production is carried out on a daily basis.

Exam insight

In order to assess possible responses to change, you need to identify the various advantages and disadvantages of each option, as well as their significance to the business in the case study.

Changes to strategy

Possible changes include:
- **Change the size of the workforce** – workforce planning is used by businesses to identify future human resources needs. An expanding business is likely to need more workers, whereas a firm that is contracting will probably need to shed some of its workforce. Either of these changes will take time to implement.
- **Retrain existing workers** – workforce planning can also be used to ensure workers have the necessary skills. Retraining existing workers can be more effective than recruiting new staff, by giving them new skills but continuing to make use of their experience within the firm. Showing commitment to employees by investing in them can also increase motivation levels.
- **Increase workforce flexibility** – a flexible workforce is achieved by giving workers skills that can be adapted easily to change. It may be helpful to adopt what Charles Handy calls the 'Shamrock' approach:
  1 A small number of permanent, 'core' staff, performing roles that are vital to the business.
  2 Peripheral workers, including those employed on a temporary, fixed-contract basis.
  3 Subcontracted staff to complete specialist tasks or functions.

AQA Business Studies for A2 Revision Guide

A* insight

Many terms in business mean different things at different times to different people. Productivity is one such term; workforce flexibility is another. If you were an employer, you might see it as your right to hire and fire as you see fit, and to reshuffle your staff as you wish. Yet if you are a 28-year-old with a mortgage and a couple of kids, you need security and stability. And if you have been at the firm for ten years, you may feel you have a moral right to be treated as someone who has built the business to where it is today. One person's flexibility may be another person's insecurity. Just because something is right for the business doesn't make it right morally.

Changes to financial strategy

Possible changes include:

- **Raise additional finance** – responding to any kind of change is likely to need funding. Firms must carefully consider the choices available to them, before choosing an appropriate source. For example, a firm that is already highly geared may struggle to meet the repayments on new and existing loans if interest rates go up.
- **Improve financial stability** – it is much easier for a business to cope with high levels of debt and low levels of liquidity when the economy is buoyant and sales are rising. However, if demand is unstable or likely to be affected by recession, adopting a financial strategy that increases liquidity and creates low levels of gearing is much less risky.
- **Return cash to shareholders** – reducing the level of share capital can help a business to improve its return on capital employed (ROCE) figures, without the need to increase profit levels. However, using cash to buy back shares reduces liquidity and may increase gearing. Many of the banks that collapsed in 2007–2009 had returned cash to their shareholders a few years earlier. So when the businesses needed the cash (for that 'rainy day') they didn't have it.

Application

Discount supermarket Aldi has attempted to distance itself from other budget chains by moving 'upmarket'. The company's expansion in the UK has increasingly focused on choosing middle-class locations and including product lines such as crayfish tails and Italian ham, in order to attract more affluent customers. For a number of years, the no-frills supermarket was mainly associated with customers on low incomes.

However, the effects of recession and rising energy bills have eroded the incomes of many households across the country, meaning that 50% of new Aldi customers are from social classes ABC1. Aldi, which has 410 stores in the UK and a market share of 2.3%, is aiming to be operating 1,500 outlets in the country by 2013.

Sources: BusinessWeek, www.bbc.co.uk

Themes for evaluation

You may be asked to suggest and assess a number of potential responses that a business could make to changes that have occurred, then make a judgement as to which would be the most appropriate. Commenting on the timing of a response may also be needed – in some cases a speedy response may help a firm stay ahead of its competitors but, in other cases, it may be better to be cautious and adopt a 'wait and see' approach.

Key terms

Liquidity – the ability of a firm to meet its debts in the short term, by keeping sufficient assets in the form of cash or near-cash resources.

Workforce planning – a process that aims to ensure a business has the right number of workers with the right skills and abilities to meet its needs.

Return on capital employed (ROCE) – the return that a business is able to generate on the long-term capital employed in the business, expressed in percentage terms.

Test yourself (15 marks)

1. Briefly explain the difference between a tactical and a structural change. (3)
2. Analyse one advantage and one disadvantage for a low-cost clothes retailer such as Primark of attempting to change its image by launching a more expensive range of brands. (4)
3. Outline two reasons why a firm might choose to change its location. (2)
4. Examine one benefit for a firm from retraining existing workers, rather than recruiting new staff. (3)
5. Identify three factors that a firm should consider when deciding on sources of funds to finance changes in strategy. (3)

Introduction

Ethics are the moral principles and guidelines that underpin decision-making. For a business, ethical behaviour involves doing what is morally acceptable, rather than just acting within the law. An ethical decision may involve choosing an option that best serves the interests of the various stakeholders of a business, even though this may reduce the level of profits made. For example, a manufacturer might choose to remain in the UK, rather than move to a lower-cost location overseas, in order to safeguard the jobs of its employees.

Traditionally, managers within a firm were expected to act on behalf of the shareholders of the business, putting their interests and the need to make profit before all other considerations. This approach, known as the shareholder concept, has been challenged in recent years by the view that managers have responsibilities to all of their stakeholders, including employees, customers, suppliers and the wider community.

Creating a culture of ethical behaviour

Some firms act in a socially responsible way because their owners, managers and employees genuinely want to do so. Companies such as The Body Shop and One Water have taken a strong ethical stance since start-up, reflecting the views of their founders and recruiting staff with the same beliefs and attitudes. Other businesses have attempted to change their culture in response to increasing pressures within the external environment. This pressure may result from customer expectations that firms will become more ethical or from the activities of pressure groups.

Changing organisational culture can, however, be a difficult and long drawn-out process. Not only do all staff need to accept the need to behave ethically, but they also have to reach agreement as to what ethical behaviour actually is. The first step is to identify and clarify the ethical issues that employees are likely to encounter. It may also help to look at the approaches adopted by other businesses and copy best practice. Training is often used to instill corporate ethics on an individual level and to ensure that all employees have the knowledge and skills to make the same ethical decisions.

Application

Although there is no doubting the general interest in ethical business, there is no room for complacency. Recent years have seen a remarkable number of cases of deeply unethical business practices by British companies (and politicians). Among recent business cases of unethical practice have been:
- BP's safety and environmental record in America.
- Trafigura's toxic waste scandal in the Ivory Coast.
- Many cases of illegal price-fixing, leading to huge fines for companies such as British Airways and Pilkington Glass.
- Cases of bribery in order to win valuable contracts, as in the case of Britain's largest manufacturer of military equipment.

Ethical codes of practice

The purpose of an ethical code of practice is to improve the behaviour and image of a firm, by outlining the ways in which it should respond whenever its corporate values are challenged. An ethical code usually begins by clarifying exactly what these values are. The exact nature of the ethical code depends on the business concerned and the environment in which it operates. It may, for example, involve making commitments to treating customers, suppliers and competitors fairly, or minimising the impact of its activities on the environment. Firms usually publish their ethical codes of practice in order to confirm their commitment to ethical behaviour, as this can have significant marketing benefits.

Benefits of behaving ethically

Firms can benefit from behaving ethically in a number of ways, including:
- **Marketing benefits** – firms such as Innocent Drinks have built their public image around their ethical stance; this can differentiate them from competitors and become the focus of their marketing strategies.
- **Human resource benefits** – employees are more likely to prefer working for a business that recognises their needs and treats them well. Having a reputation as a caring employer can make recruitment more effective by improving the quality of candidates attracted to vacancies. It

should also result in low levels of labour turnover, reducing recruitment and training costs.

Drawbacks of behaving ethically

These may include:

- **Reduced profits** – behaving in a socially responsible manner may mean higher wages and more training for employees, paying higher prices to suppliers and investing in new equipment and processes to reduce damage to the environment. It may also mean turning down highly-profitable investment opportunities, if these projects involve behaving in a way that conflicts with a firm's ethical principles.
- **Conflicts with other business policies** – firms with a tradition of democratic management and decentralisation may find it difficult to introduce more ethical policies across the whole organisation, unless there is general support for such a move.

Application

In April 2009, Innocent Drinks became the latest ethical business to sell a stake of its company to a much larger organisation. Innocent received £30 million from fizzy drinks giant, Coca-Cola, in exchange for a 30% share of the business. Innocent's owners and co-founders – Richard Reed, Jon Wright and Adam Bolan – insisted that the link-up would not affect its principles or products, despite past criticisms against Coca-Cola for producing unhealthy drinks and exploitation of workers and the environment. According to Reed, 'We'll just have more resources to keep doing what we care about – bringing natural healthy foods to more people using environmentally friendly ingredients and packaging'.

Source: The London Evening Standard

Themes for evaluation

Behaving ethically may seem like a noble goal but, for most businesses, the decision is likely to depend on the extent to which profit levels will be affected by such a move. Any change in strategy results in increased costs, at least in the short term. You may be expected, therefore, to assess the extent to which these costs will be offset by longer-term benefits.

Exam insight

Assessing whether or not a firm should become more ethical requires a clear understanding of the business, the attitude of its owners, its employees, its customers and its competitors. For example, are shareholders willing to accept lower returns, at least in the short term? Are employees likely to be supportive and respond positively? Do customers expect the firm to behave ethically or are they more interested in low prices?

A* Insight

A* students understand the theory at either end of a 'on the one hand … on the other hand' argument. But they also have the subtlety to move beyond this towards understanding shades of grey. Although ethics can be seen as a straightforward case of right and wrong, the business world may make this very difficult. Price fixing is unethical (and illegal), but what if it's the only way to enable a business with 500 employees to survive a recession? There is reason to have sympathy with a person having to make that decision.

Key terms

Ethics – the moral principles and guidelines that underpin business decision-making.

Pressure group – when people with a common interest come together and form an organisation to promote that interest.

Shareholder concept – the view that the main responsibility of managers is to protect and promote the interests of the owners of a business, the shareholders.

Stakeholder – individuals or groups, such as owners, employees or customers, that have an interest in how a business is run.

Stakeholder concept – the view that managers have responsibilities to all of the stakeholder groups involved in the business, not just the shareholders.

Test yourself (15 marks)

1 What is meant by 'ethical behaviour'? (2)
2 Briefly explain the difference between the shareholder concept and the stakeholder concept. (3)
3 Outline three steps that a firm could take when attempting to adopt a more ethical culture. (3)
4 What is an ethical code of practice? (2)
5 Examine one likely benefit and one possible drawback for a firm of adopting ethical policies. (5)

Unit 39 Business and the environment

Introduction

Growing concern about the environment among politicians, pressure groups and consumers in recent years has encouraged an increasing number of firms to consider more closely the environmental impact of their activities. Many businesses have already put in place policies designed to minimise environmental damage caused by their operations and maximise the marketing benefits of being seen to do so.

Environmental issues affecting firms

These include:
- **Pollution** – this does not just refer to the dumping of waste chemicals into the ground, atmosphere, rivers and oceans but also includes factors such as excessive noise and congestion. As households become more and more wealthy, they become more concerned about the impact of industrial growth on the quality of life. Excessive quantities of carbon dioxide, produced by burning fossil fuels such as coal and oil, has been accepted as a key contributor to global warming. In response to this, many firms now publish details about their 'carbon footprint', i.e., the amount of carbon dioxide produced by their operations, along with the steps taken to offset this production.
- **Sustainable development** – excessive use of non-renewable resources such as coal, oil and natural gas has forced firms to consider alternatives for when these resources run out.
- **Recycling** – finding ways of using resources over and over again has reduced the rate of depletion of non-renewable resources and also helped, in some cases, to reduce costs.

Environmental audits

This is an independent check on the environmental impact of a firm's activities, taking into account factors such as pollution emissions, wastage levels and recycling policies. If the results are published, the public is able to judge the progress firms are making towards achieving environmental targets. It creates an incentive for the firm concerned to achieve any targets set, as well as generating a positive image if targets are met. As environmental audits are voluntary,

it may be that they are published only by firms that can claim to perform well. Pressure groups such as Greenpeace believe that environmental audits should be statutory, i.e. a legal requirement for all plcs.

The impact of the environment on operations

The decision to become more environmentally friendly has a number of implications for operations. These include:
- **The materials used in production** – finite resources used as part of the production process will need to be switched, wherever possible, to those that are renewable. This is likely to impose additional, if temporary, costs on firms.
- **Production processes** – firms may need to adopt production processes that generate less pollution, that are more energy efficient, or use sources that can be replenished. Implementing and using these new methods is likely to increase costs.

The impact of the environment on marketing

Environmental issues are also likely to have an impact on a firm's marketing strategies. A green image may well lead to increased sales and stronger brand loyalty, possibly allowing the firm concerned to recoup any additional costs incurred by charging higher prices. However, just as projecting an image of being environmentally friendly can boost the market standing of a business, these benefits can be eroded overnight if any contradictory evidence is uncovered. Indeed, many business commentators agree that green credentials are now more of a requirement than an advantage for all products.

Application

Entrepreneur James Dyson has revealed his latest invention – a bladeless fan which acts as an environmentally-friendly alternative to air conditioning. According to Mr Dyson, 'If only we could open a window and use a fan then we would be saving a huge amount of electricity, stopping the emission of HFCs and having a much healthier environment.' The fan is said to run on ⅟₅₀th of the electricity used by conventional air conditioning systems.

Source: The Press Association

Themes for evaluation

Showing evaluation may require you to make recommendations as to how a firm can best adjust its operations in order to become more environmentally friendly or an assessment of the likely benefits and costs of doing so.

Exam insight

You need to consider carefully the ways in which a business could introduce changes that could benefit the environment. You also need to attempt to identify and measure the benefits and costs involved in doing so.

A* insight

A useful term to consider is the word 'greenwash'. It means whitewash in the context of the environment, i.e. to pretend to be green. The most blatant version of this was when BP changed its logo to a combination of sunny yellow and green, and changed the stated meaning of BP from British Petroleum to 'Beyond Petroleum'. It is right to be sceptical about business claims regarding the environment. Beware, though, of sounding cynical.

Key Terms

Environmental audit – an independent check on the environmental impact of a firm's activities, including factors such as pollution emissions, wastage levels and recycling practices.
Recycling – sorting out products so that they can be collected and reused, in order to reduce the quantity of raw materials used in the production process.
Sustainable development – relying on production processes that can be continued into the long-term future, i.e., that do not depend on the use of finite resources, such as oil and natural gas.

Test yourself (15 marks)

1 Examine two reasons why many firms have decided to adopt environmentally-friendly practices. (4)
2 Identify three environmental issues that businesses now face. (3)
3 What is meant by an environmental audit? (2)
4 Outline one benefit and one drawback for a firm of publishing its environmental audits. (2)
5 Examine two implications for a firm's operations of becoming more environmentally friendly. (4)

Business and the environment

Unit 40 Business and the technological environment

Introduction

In many sectors of business, technological change is a constant, affecting both products and processes. This creates both opportunities and threats for businesses. The developments affect what is being produced (product) and also how it is being made (process). More and more new products are being produced more quickly and at higher levels of quality than ever before, increasing the degree of competition within the marketplace. In many markets, product life cycles are becoming shorter. This means businesses are forced to invest greater sums in new product development, but have a shorter length of time in which to generate the revenues needed to recoup this investment.

Increasing the level of technology used in production can reduce unit costs significantly, but is expensive to acquire and managers may lack the funds to keep up with the latest developments. However, those firms who choose to ignore the latest technological developments are likely to get left behind by rivals that do adopt it. The key issue is timing. New technology can become out-of-date very quickly but taking too long to respond can lead to a loss of competitiveness.

The impact of technological change on business

- **The impact on operations** – one of the main causes of this increasingly rapid rate of change is the actual use of technology within industry. Computer-aided design (CAD) and computer-aided manufacturing (CAM) have both helped to significantly reduce the time taken to develop new products and identify new ways of producing them more quickly, improving quality at the same time. Increasingly sophisticated machines are developed to carry out more complex tasks previously done by workers, increasing productivity, lowering waste levels and reducing costs. The speed and quality of communications has also been improved by technological developments such as video-conferencing and email.
- **The impact on marketing** – technology has not just allowed businesses to improve existing goods and services but has created a vast number of brand new products, including MP3 players, laptops, satellite navigation systems and portable

games stations. By reducing the costs of production of these products, technology allowed them to become much more affordable, boosting demand and creating mass markets across the world. The internet has provided firms with a relatively cheap and effective means of promotion, while developments such as broadband have made it much easier for customers to shop online.
- **The impact on human relations** – workers may be affected by technological change in a number of ways. Updating computer systems, for example, may require staff to retrain. More widespread changes, such as an increase in the level of automation, may lead to workers having to take on new roles and responsibilities, or even being made redundant. Rapid or major changes are likely to meet with resistance from staff (managers and workers), particularly if they do not understand why change is taking place and feel that they will be worse off as a result.

A* insight

When there is an exam question on new technology, most students write generalisations. It is as if every firm is the same as Apple or Nintendo. Yet there are many firms that operate in markets that are very slow-moving. Cadbury's Dairy Milk has been a thing of beauty and wonder for more than 100 years. The product has changed little and the process of manufacture changes relatively little, decade by decade. Even the 'internal combustion engine' that powers almost all the world's cars has been around for a century. Yes, technological change can be hugely important, but you must apply a critical eye to the circumstances of each business.

Business responses to technological change

The rate of technological change is likely to continue to speed up in the future, especially for those firms operating in high-technology markets. Whether this leads to benefits or problems for a business depends on the ability to predict the nature of the changes and the ability to react to them. Firms are faced with enormous pressures to keep up with technological change, in order to satisfy changing customer needs and to reduce costs. However, there are reasons to think carefully about rushing to support every technological change:

- Investment in research and development can drain a firm's resources. Some firms may struggle to raise the funds needed to purchase new technology and develop new products. In particular, financing investment in new products and technological processes by borrowing can be risky, given that it may take years before any real benefits are derived. Given that organisations have finite resources, managers need to consider carefully the impact of technological improvement on other areas of the business, such as staff training.
- New technology may not always work effectively from the outset. New products that do not deliver their promises can lead to customer disappointment that may affect future sales and have a knock-on effect on demand for other products produced by a business. There may be teething problems with newly-installed machinery and workers may take time to learn new production methods. Managers may have to accept lower productivity and higher wastage levels, at least in the short term, as a result.

Application

Telecommunications firm, BT, has claimed that an additional 1.5 million homes will benefit from super-fast broadband by 2013. The company had previously claimed that it could only supply the fibre-to-the-premises (FTTP) technology to one million homes in new-build sites, but now says it has found new ways to make it more widely available and much cheaper to provide. FTTP technology can deliver speeds of 100Mbps (megabits per second). The top speed of its slower fibre-to-the-cabinet (FTTC) is only 50Mbps. However, BT faces stiff competition from a number of other companies, including Virgin Media, which has trialled speeds of up to 200Mbps.

Source: www.bbc.co.uk

Themes for evaluation

This is likely to involve making a judgement on the extent to which technological advances are likely to impact on a business. It may create scope for reducing costs or create opportunities for new products or it could threaten the survival of a business or entire industry. Alternatively, you might be asked to consider the potential difficulties that a firm could face in attempting to adopt new technology and evaluate possible solutions to these problems.

Exam insight

You need to ensure that you have a clear understanding of exactly how a business is likely to be affected by technological change, as well as whether these changes are beneficial or not. You also need to identify any possible reasons why the firm concerned might find it difficult to respond positively to technological change – for example, does it have the necessary financial resources and are employees likely to be resistant?

Key terms

Computer-aided design (CAD) – software that allows the development, storage and modification of product designs in a digital format.

Computer-aided manufacture (CAM) – using computers in various aspects of manufacturing, carrying out production tasks but also in areas such as stock ordering and control.

Test yourself (20 marks)

1 Outline two ways in which technology can improve a firm's operations. (4)
2 Describe two ways in which technology can improve a firm's marketing strategies. (4)
3 Examine two implications of the impact of technology on the life cycle of high-tech goods, such as mobile phones and MP3 players. (6)
4 Suggest one reason why small firms in particular might struggle to keep up with technological advances in operations. (2)
5 Suggest two reasons why workers might be resistant to a firm's decision to adopt new technology. (4)

Business and the technological environment

Unit 41 Impact of competitive and market structure

Introduction

A competitive market is one where there is intense rivalry between competing businesses. The more firms there are within the market, the more intense the rivalry is likely to be. In addition, the level of competition is also influenced by the share of the market controlled by the different firms operating within it.

The degree of competition has a direct impact on prices and profits – the fiercer the competition, the greater the pressure to push prices down in order to attract custom. Unless firms can improve efficiency and reduce costs in line with price reductions, profit margins are reduced. They may attempt, therefore, to take action to differentiate themselves from other firms in the market by creating strong brands with unique selling points that appeal to customers by satisfying their needs more effectively. They may also take steps to reduce or even eliminate the competition by using tactics such as **predatory pricing**.

The degree of competition in a market

- **One dominant business** – the level of competition in markets that are dominated by a single business tends to be relatively low. Dominant or **monopoly** firms are able to set prices within the market that all other firms are likely to follow. Firms may achieve a dominant position by simply being more successful in meeting customer needs and growing organically. Others may reach a dominant position by merging with or taking over other successful firms within the market.
- **A few firms in the market – oligopoly** is the term used to describe a market that consists of a few dominant firms. The level of competition in such markets can be fierce but often focuses on non-price methods, such as branding and promotion. Oligopolies can usually avoid price wars that simply result in reduced revenues for all the firms involved.
- **Fiercely competitive markets** – these are likely to be made up of hundreds of relatively small firms who compete actively against each other to maintain or increase market share. The degree of differentiation between products and businesses is crucial. Firms producing products with little, if any,

differentiation from rivals are likely to compete on the basis of price. This means cost-cutting becomes the most important factor in determining whether or not a product sells.

Changes in the competitive structure of a market

- **New competitors** – firms are usually tempted into new markets by opportunities to earn significant levels of profit. Strategies are likely to be based on the introduction of a brand new product, significant improvements to existing product lines or simply undercutting competitors by charging lower prices.
- **The emergence of a dominant firm** – a dominant business is one that has a high market share, relative to other firms in the same market. The level of competition in markets with one dominant business tends to be low, with the dominant firm setting prices that smaller firms usually follow. This degree of market power may result from organic growth achieved over a period of time. Alternatively, a merger or takeover between two firms in the same market and at the same stage of production leads to an increase in market concentration and a reduction in the level of competition.
- **Changes in customers' buying power** – markets tend to become more competitive during recessions when the level of consumer spending tends to fall. Firms are likely to cut prices and run more aggressive promotional campaigns in order to attract the customers that remain. Firms do not need to compete as aggressively to win sales when consumer spending is increasing and markets are expanding.
- **Changes in suppliers' selling power** – the selling power of suppliers is affected by costs, such as raw materials and wages. Rising costs make it less profitable to supply goods and services, so firms tend to supply less. The level of competition in a market is likely to increase if market supply decreases but the level of demand remains unchanged.
- **Market-sharing agreements** – firms within a market may agree to cooperate with each other, rather than compete against each other, by forming a cartel. Cartels lead to market conditions similar to those created by a monopoly, where the degree of competition is reduced.

Students tend to overestimate the security involved in a strong market position. In fact remarkably few companies survive as the dominant producer from one generation to the next. Your parents' first car was probably made in Britain by Austin Rover, which once held 50% of the UK car market. It died several years ago. And their introduction to yoghurt was probably a brand called Ski, which was the Muller of its day. Ski's market share has gone from 60% to less than 5%.

Andy Grove, boss of the dominant Intel microprocessor business, famously said that: 'Only the paranoid survive'. So beware of assuming that dominant businesses naturally stay dominant. They have to work at it.

Business responses to a changing competitive environment

A business faced with increasing competition within its market will be forced to react in order to protect its market share. Typical responses include:

- **Price cutting** – price is an important determinant of demand and so firms may try to retain customers by undercutting the prices charged by rivals. Falling prices can, however, reduce profitability, so a business may also attempt to reduce costs in line with price cuts in order to maintain profit margins. Predatory pricing is sometimes used to drive other firms out of the market completely by reducing prices to a point where they are unable to compete.
- **Increased product differentiation** – non-price competition involves making products stand out from rivals by creating a strong brand image or a unique design or by improving quality. The greater the degree of differentiation, the more likely customers will view the firm as the sole supplier of a unique product, rather than one of many firms selling similar goods or services.
- **Entering new markets** – a market may become so saturated with competing firms and products that the scope for further growth is negligible. Holding on to market share and taking sales from rivals requires increasing levels of promotional expenditure and further price cuts, placing greater pressure on profit margins. In such cases, a firm may decide to look for new markets, such as those located overseas, with less competition and offering greater opportunities for sales growth.
- **Takeovers of rivals** – one way of dealing with a successful rival is to take them over, reducing the degree of competition and increasing market share overnight. Takeovers and mergers may, however, be prevented by the government if they are expected to reduce the level of competition significantly.

Application

In 2007, six firms, including retailers Sainsbury's and Asda, were fined a total of £116 million by the Office of Fair Trading (OFT) after admitting to fixing the prices of a number of dairy products. The OFT claimed that the collusion had cost UK consumers an additional £270 million. According to its estimates, shoppers had been charged an extra three pence for a pint of milk and around 15 pence extra for a quarter-pound of cheese.

Source: www.bbc.co.uk

Themes for evaluation

You may be asked to suggest and justify an appropriate strategy that a business could adopt in response to an increase in competition within the marketplace. Remember that there is always the option of doing nothing, but the cost of winning back lost sales tends to be much higher than attempting to maintain existing customer loyalty.

Exam insight

The response chosen by a firm to an increase in competition will depend, at least to some extent, on its situation and the resources available. For example, a firm operating on tight profit margins may not be able to afford further price cuts.

Key terms

Monopoly – a situation where a market is dominated by one large firm.
Oligopoly – a market dominated by a small number of very large firms.
Predatory pricing – where a firm prices its products at such low levels that competitors are forced out of the market.

Test yourself (20 marks)

1 Describe two factors that influence the degree of competition within a market. (4)
2 Explain what is meant by a monopoly. (3)
3 Explain why the dominant firms in an oligopoly are more likely to use non-price competition than price cutting to maintain or increase their market share. (3)
4 Outline two ways in which a firm can become more dominant within its market. (4)
5 Analyse two ways in which a firm could respond to an increase in competition within its market. (6)

Unit 42 Internal and external growth: takeovers and mergers

AQA Business Studies for A2 Revision Guide

Organic growth

Organic growth is from within the business, i.e. it is internal growth. This occurs when a firm expands in response to increasing demand for its products. In order to sell more, it has to produce more, so needs more labour and capital. Growth from within is usually considered a relatively safe form of growth. This is because:
- finance is more likely to come from retained profits than borrowing
- the firm has time to adjust gradually and adopt an appropriate internal structure.

However, organic growth usually occurs at a relatively slow pace. A firm that relies on organic growth may lack the capacity to deal with a sudden surge in demand, missing out on opportunities due to a lack of resources.

Takeovers and mergers

A firm must acquire at least 51% of the share capital of another company in order to complete a takeover and gain control of its management. The management of the company that is subject to a takeover may be supportive of the move or they may try to prevent it (known as a hostile takeover). A merger, on the other hand, occurs when the management and shareholders of two separate companies agree to come together and create a new organisation under a common board of directors.

Reasons for takeovers and mergers

These include:
- **Growth** – merger or takeover allows growth to be achieved much more quickly than by relying on organic growth.
- **Cost savings** – operating on a larger scale may lead to economies of scale, reducing unit costs. Mergers or takeovers may produce **synergies**, i.e., the benefits of having lower costs and higher profits than those that were generated by the two separate organizations.
- **Increased market power** – takeover or merger involving two firms in the same industry reduces the level of competition. This can create opportunities to increase prices and generate higher profits.
- **Diversification** – merging or taking over a business operating in another market can reduce

a firm's dependence on current customers and products. The firm concerned will already be established in the market and selling products successfully, saving the time and money that would have been needed to do this from scratch.

A* Insight

Many students know that the majority of takeovers are unsuccessful – leading to the question: why do it? Fewer can deal with the key analysis needed of the relationship between quantitative and qualitative factors. By definition, quantitative factors can be calculated and therefore treated as 'real'. For example, if two producers of instant coffee merge, the combined buying power might cut variable costs by 10%. Much harder is to judge the diseconomies of scale that – history shows – are likely to emerge. How can you calculate the effect of poorer communications or lower motivation? You cannot, therefore bosses tend to approach takeovers with qualitative factors assumed away ('I'm a great boss, so I'll handle the communication issue'). It is wise to be highly sceptical of the motives and the assumptions involved in every takeover bid.

Types of business integration

Integration is the general term used to refer to a situation where two or more firms come together, as in the case of takeover or merger. It can take the form of any of the following:
- **Horizontal integration** – where two firms at the same stage of production come together, e.g. the takeover of one supermarket by another. This type of integration offers a number of potential benefits. The reduction in competition can lead to increased market power, although this, in turn, may trigger an investigation by the Competition Commission, which has the power to prevent the move from going ahead. Another benefit may be that significant economies of scale are generated, reducing unit costs and creating opportunities to reduce prices and become more competitive.
- **Vertical integration** – this takes place when one firm merges with or takes over another firm at a different stage of production. Backward vertical integration occurs when a firm buys out a supplier. This can help to improve operations by increasing

control over the quality of supplies and the timing of their delivery. It can also help to reduce costs by eliminating suppliers' profit margins. However, managers and workers within the supplier division may grow complacent, once the need to compete for orders disappears, leading to rising costs and falling quality levels. Forward vertical integration involves buying out a customer. This would give a producer direct contact with its customers and also allow it to absorb retailers' margins, leading to higher profits.

- **Conglomerate integration** – this occurs when two businesses from completely different industries come together. No obvious connection between the firms exists. The main reasons for this type of integration are to achieve rapid growth and to diversify. However, research would seem to indicate that conglomerates have the lowest chances of success. This is likely to be because managers at the takeover company will have no knowledge of the market and products of the firm it has taken over. This lack of experience is likely to reduce the effectiveness of decision-making, increasing the risks of failure.

Retrenchment and demergers

A business may decide that it has grown too big and would benefit from operating on a smaller scale. Large firms often experience problems with communication and coordination, as well as falling levels of employee motivation. In such cases, managers may decide to implement a policy of retrenchment. This involves taking steps to reduce capacity by selling off plant and equipment and making workers redundant.

Firms that have been involved in past mergers are often disappointed with the results. Expected synergies, falling unit costs and increased profits may fail to materialise in practice. It takes time to fuse together different organisational cultures, and attempts to force through changes are likely to create conflict, particularly if large-scale redeployment or redundancies are implemented. Reversing the process is known as demerger. Having expanded into a number of different areas, a business may decide to concentrate its resources on the one area that is the most profitable, rather than spreading resources thinly over a number of products and markets. Selling off parts of the business can also help to generate finance required to pay off existing debts or to fund future investment.

Application

Historic Scottish textile manufacturer, Todd & Duncan, was sold by its owners, Dawson International, to a Chinese company in 2009 for £6.1 million. The Kinross-based firm has been spinning cashmere for over 140 years and supplies yarn to some of the world s most famous fashion houses, including Chanel, Gucci and Prada. The deal was expected to secure 200 jobs at the company.

Source: www.bbc.co.uk

Themes for evaluation

You may be asked to assess the potential benefits and risks involved in growth. This could require you to compare the costs and benefits of growth via integration, as opposed to organic growth, or to make an assessment of the merits and demerits of a specific takeover or merger. Alternatively, you could be required to consider the advantages and disadvantages of a firm reducing its size, either by retrenchment or demerger.

Exam insight

One possible approach to evaluating the impact of a takeover or merger is to consider the impact on various stakeholder groups. How will the shareholders in each company be affected? What groups are most likely to benefit or suffer and how will this affect performance?

Key terms

Demerger – when a firm is split into two or more separate companies.
Integration – the bringing together of two or more companies, either via takeover or merger.
Retrenchment – reducing the level of capacity within a business by selling off assets and / or making workers redundant.
Synergies – when the benefits created by integrating different firms are greater than the sum of the parts, i.e., 2+2=5.

Test yourself (20 marks)

1. Outline one benefit and one drawback of organic growth for a business. (4)
2. Give two reasons why a firm might choose to expand via integration rather than by internal growth. (4)
3. Explain what is meant by horizontal integration. (2)
4. Explain the difference between backward vertical integration and forward vertical integration. (4)
5. What does conglomerate integration involve? (2)
6. Suggest two reasons why a firm might decide to reduce the scale of its operations. (4)

Managers spend much of their time focusing on internal issues within their businesses. Yet the external environment is just as, if not more, likely to influence performance in the long term. When planning for the future, a business needs to assess external opportunities and threats, as well as the internal strengths and weaknesses that may exist. PEST analysis gives firms a framework for examining the impact of the various external factors – both opportunities and threats – that could influence a business. It examines the political, economic, social and technological factors that could impact on a firm:

● **Political factors** – government policies have a direct impact on business activities. The expansion of the EU has opened up new markets and brought in skilled staff from Eastern Europe. It has helped British economic growth and therefore aided UK businesses. Changes in legislation may curtail some business activities completely or provoke a rethink in operations.

● **Economic factors** – the business cycle has a major impact on business. Recessions reduce the level of economic activity, leading to lower rates of inflation and higher unemployment. Falling exchange rates make it easier for firms to export but increases the costs of those firms that rely on imports.

● **Social factors** – social changes can have a significant impact on business. For example, increasing interest in healthier lifestyles has boosted demand for some food products at the expense of others. It has also created huge new markets, from leisure centres to magazines (the top-selling men's magazine is now *Men's Health*).

● **Technological factors** – scientific developments lead to the creation of new products and production processes, but also present challenges to existing practices. The cost of producing existing products can be reduced and brand new markets can be created. However, some products and processes can be made obsolete by technological advances.

Exam insight

All business decisions are about the future. Some PEST changes are known in advance. Businesses knew for two years that Romania was to join the EU in 2007 (which would increase consumers' living standards and therefore spending). Therefore businesses could plan and prepare, e.g. open Pizza Express restaurants in the capital city. Far more often, though, the future is completely unknown. Organic food went from hero to zero in Britain in the course of 2008. So businesses must plan for the future in the knowledge that shock surprises will happen. Therefore their financial position should always be liquid enough to deal with an unexpected crisis.

Test yourself (80 marks)

1 Explain what is meant by 'the business cycle'. (2)
2 Outline two effects of falling inflation on UK businesses. (4)
3 Analyse one effect of increasing unemployment on a car manufacturer based in the UK. (3)
4 Describe the main effects of a rise in the value of the pound against the euro for UK firms. (3)
5 Briefly explain the difference between fiscal policy and monetary policy. (3)
6 Explain what is meant by 'globalisation'. (2)
7 Describe two benefits for UK firms of the increasing trend towards globalisation. (4)
8 Outline two challenges for UK firms from globalisation. (4)
9 Explain what is meant by 'an emerging economy'. (2)
10 Examine one benefit and one drawback for a firm from becoming involved in an emerging economy. (4)
11 Describe one possible benefit and one possible drawback for a UK supermarket chain from a further expansion in EU membership. (4)
12 Analyse two ways in which employment legislation acts as a constraint on UK firms. (6)
13 Outline two possible consequences for a firm that chooses to ignore health and safety legislation. (4)
14 Outline one financial strategy that a business could adopt in the face of an economic downturn. (3)

15 Describe one operational strategy and one marketing strategy that a UK footwear manufacturer could adopt to deal with an increase in competition from foreign firms based in China. (4)

16 What is meant by 'business ethics'? (2)

17 Examine one advantage and one disadvantage to a firm of behaving more ethically in its treatment of suppliers. (4)

18 Identify two environmental issues facing businesses. (2)

19 Outline one benefit and one drawback for a firm of carrying out an annual environmental audit. (4)

20 Identify two ways in which technology can improve the efficiency of a firm's operations. (2)

21 Give two reasons why a business may decide not to respond to an increase in competition by cutting prices. (2)

22 Explain the difference between internal and external growth. (2)

23 Briefly explain one advantage and one disadvantage of horizontal integration. (4)

24 Using examples, explain the difference between forward vertical integration and backward vertical integration. (3)

25 Explain what is meant by conglomerate integration. (3)

Case study – is recovery in sight for the UK economy?

Despite optimism that the UK economy would have begun to grow again during the second half of the year, data published in the third quarter of 2009 indicated that it was still in recession. Growing confidence based on predictions of an increase of 0.3% in UK Gross Domestic Product (GDP) between July and September, followed by a further rise of 0.4% between October and December, suffered a setback when it was revealed that industrial output fell unexpectedly in August by 2.5% on the previous month. The number of unemployed people in the UK rose by 88,000 during the three months to August 2009, to reach a total of 2.47 million, the highest figure for 14 years, although the rate of increase was slower than that of previous months. The CBI has predicted that unemployment figures will peak at three million during the second half of 2010. Fears about job losses, low wage increases and, in many cases, wage freezes have encouraged consumers to cut back on spending and save more in order to start paying back record levels of debt. Sharp cutbacks in business investment and government spending have also contributed to the fall in demand and the rise in unemployment in the UK.

The data undermined hopes that the UK would follow trading partners, France and Germany, into recovery. The two biggest EU economies both registered increases in GDP of 0.3% in the three months to June 2009, the first time either had experienced any economic growth since the first quarter of 2008. Official figures released by the Chinese government confirm a slowdown in the decline of exports from the country, suggesting that world demand is beginning to recover. Chinese exports fell by just over 15% in September 2009, the smallest fall since the beginning of the year. Economic growth in China, currently the world's third largest economy, increased from 6.1% in the first quarter to 7.9% in the second quarter of 2009.

Official statistics for the UK also showed a continuing decline in the rate of UK inflation during the autumn of 2009. The Consumer Prices Index (CPI) fell from 1.6% in August to 1.1% in September – its lowest level since September 2004. Another key measure of inflation, the Retail Prices Index (RPI), fell to −1.4% from −1.3% over the same period. The announcement of the figures caused a further weakening of the exchange rate. The value of sterling fell to 1.06, its lowest level for six months against the euro, and to $1.57, a five-month low against the dollar. Despite these figures, the Bank of England left UK interest rates unchanged at 0.5% for the seventh consecutive month.

Questions (40 marks)

1 Briefly explain the following terms
   a) Gross Domestic Product
   b) Inflation
   c) Exchange rate. (6 marks)

2 Examine the main causes of the rising level of UK unemployment during 2009. (10 marks)

3 Analyse two implications for UK businesses of the falling levels of inflation experienced during 2009. (10 marks)

4 Assess the decision of a UK manufacturer of high-quality food products to concentrate on developing overseas sales, rather than focus on the UK market during the period 2009/10. (14 marks)

7 Managing change

Unit 44 Causes of and planning for change

What?

Businesses operate in a world that is constantly changing and they also have internal pressures that change over time. The better that change can be foreseen, planned for and managed, the more able the business should be to cope with those changes.

It is natural to assume that once a company becomes the biggest in its market, it will stay the biggest. In fact this is not true. In recent years there have been good examples of this. General Motors was the world's biggest for more than 70 years – but was pushed aside by Toyota (now Volkswagen plans to overtake Toyota). And Sony was unchallenged for more than ten years with its Walkman brand – until Apple's iPod stole the show.

In the words of a dismal advertisement for an insurance company: 'Change Happenz'.

Internal reasons for change:
- change in business objectives
- change in the size of the organisation
- a change in leadership.

External reasons for change:
- changes in the economic climate
- changes to laws affecting the organisation
- changes in consumers' tastes, attitudes and behaviours.

Whereas internal changes can often be foreseen and hence planned for, external changes can be totally unexpected and therefore tend to be more difficult to plan for and to manage.

Why?

Internal changes are often a result of the business growing in scale. This forces the business to rethink the way it works. When a business has 2–20 staff, everyone can be involved in everything; communication occurs naturally as people overhear each other, and gossip about successes and failures. If a junior member of staff has an idea, he or she can probably pop a head round the managing director's door. But if you are Terry Leahy, boss of Tesco's 250,000 staff, none of these things apply. In the process of getting from tiny to massive, there will have to be frequent:
- changes in management
- changes in production methods

- changes in recruitment processes
- changes in personnel.

When a firm grows in size it becomes more necessary to formulate detailed policies, plans and procedures. While in a small firm, an individual may make all decisions alone and by instinct, as a firm grows and stakeholder groups expand. It becomes more necessary for decisions to be discussed before being made.

Which?

Problems with rapid growth

Growth is often a key business objective and therefore perceived as purely a positive. In fact it can cause significant problems (just ask the former shareholders in HBOS, which collapsed into the arms of Lloyds TSB during the Credit Crunch). These include:
- Lack of total knowledge/control. As the organisation grows it becomes increasingly difficult for management to have total knowledge or control. This can be disconcerting for those who are used to knowing their business inside out. In 2007 and 2008 it was clear that people paid millions to run banks had very little idea of the risks being run by their own staff.
- The need to keep changing the management structure in order to cope with ever-increasing staff levels; as new layers of management are added, there is scope both for increasing bureaucracy and for cutting off those at the top of the organisation from those at the bottom. Many bosses are guilty of following the (foolish) words of former Prime Minister Margaret Thatcher: 'Bring me solutions, not problems'. That is guaranteed to mean that the boss's first knowledge of a problem will be when it explodes.

Retrenchment

Retrenchment means to cut back. There are several ways this can be achieved.
1 **Delayering.** To remove one or more layers from the organisational hierarchy. This can lead to confusion over who is responsible for what, particularly in the short term.
2 **Recruitment freeze.** This is a rather less dramatic strategy. It means that the firm does not actually

let existing staff go but rather follows a policy of not recruiting any new staff. This may well be a first step towards retrenchment, and if conditions worsen, further and more radical steps may be taken.

3 **Offering voluntary redundancy.** This seems a more satisfactory and more humane approach to job cuts; the main problem is that the people most likely to leave are those who know they can find a job elsewhere; probably your best people.

4 **Closing an entire store or factory** which is either no longer needed or operating at a loss.

5 **Targeted redundancies.** This requires the management to analyse the performance and activities of existing staff to discover who the firm may be able to do without and who is vital to the organisation.

Application

A firm's ability to manage change depends on several factors. When reading a case study the following may be useful to consider:
a) What evidence is there that management are aware of the need for change and prepared for it?
b) Is the change positive or negative? Although growth causes several problems, do not forget that this is the objective of most businesses and the problems may be short term but the positive effects of growth may be long term (note this is not always the case).
c) The culture of the organisation. Is the culture such that change is likely to be welcomed or resisted?

Planning for change

A business has to decide, early on, whether or not it wants the process of change to be a collective, democratic effort. If it does, it has to find a way to make sure not only that the democracy is effective, but is also seen to be effective. Many staff would be inclined to cynicism – suspecting that the boss secretly knows what he or she plans to do, so discussion and debate is largely hot air.

In certain circumstances it may be that democracy is irrelevant. What may be needed is short, sharp, perhaps painful action. After all, how can you ask staff to discuss which jobs should be cut?

Application

In September 2008 business collapsed at UOE, an office supplies business. Managing Director Elliott Jacobs responded by cutting half of his sales and administration teams. Although the immediate cause was the recession, Jacobs had planned this for some time. He had decided to cut deeply, but only cut once. In this way he could persuade the remaining 105 staff that the pain was over and their jobs were safe.

Key terms

Bureaucracy – layers of management staff and processes designed to reduce the risk of mistakes (usually by slowing down decisions, or preventing them from being made).
Credit Crunch – the period between 2007 and 2009 when a banking crisis caused a worldwide economic recession.
Stakeholder groups – all those with an interest in a firm's successes, actions and failures.

Themes for evaluation

Change is an inevitable part of business and, as such, should not come as a shock but rather should be anticipated. Managers should have contingency plans in place so that all major potential changes are planned for.

However, remember that planning for change does not necessarily mean it will be successful. No matter how good the planning is, if staff are actively resistant to change it will still be difficult to implement. It is impossible to guarantee the smooth management of change so the key is planning ahead to minimise the potential barriers.

Test yourself (15 marks)

1 Outline briefly the type of change needed if:
a) Foods bought throughout Tesco's supermarkets caused a serious food poisoning outbreak, resulting in sharply falling sales.
b) An unexpected boom in the economy caused sharp sales increases at Vertu, manufacturers of super-luxury phones.
c) Customers of Danone's Activia and Actimel started to worry more about calories and less about their digestive system. (3)
2 Explain two benefits and two drawbacks of carrying out change in a democratic way. (8)
3 Briefly comment on why these quotations on change have become famous:
a) 'You cannot fight against the future', William Gladstone, Prime Minister, 1866.
b) 'If past history was all there was to the game, the richest people would be librarians', Warren Buffett, mega-rich investor, 1988. (4)

AQA Business Studies for A2 Revision Guide

Unit 45 Organisational culture

What?

Organisational culture is the very essence of an organisation. It includes the accepted norms, behaviours and ethos of the organisation and it is embodied by the people who work within it. It is something which builds, develops and changes over time.

Why?

It is important to understand because it is almost the heart and soul of an organisation. In May 2007 Newcastle United appointed a new manager. Sam Allardyce had been hugely successful at Bolton, but a few games into the 2007/08 season the fans were restless. They were used to exciting football. Allardyce was about winning games. It was a culture clash, and Allardyce lost. He was sacked after eight months.

Every business (like every school) has its own culture. Some workplaces are intense, perhaps pressurised, with a driving sense of the need to achieve. People who cannot keep up may be dismissed. This dog-eat-dog culture may be thrilling for those who succeed, and the culture may be tough but very positive. Another organisation may be ruled by fear, because someone in a position of power enjoys showing off. There is nothing positive about this state of affairs.

Culture affects almost every aspect of a business, including:
- motivation of staff
- attitudes of staff
- productivity
- desire to reach targets
- attitude to work
- ethics (such as the attitude to expenses)
- customer service.

Which?

Handy's four types of organisational culture

Charles Handy, author and business guru, wrote of four types of business culture.

Power culture

This occurs when there is a clearly defined holder of power. The culture is determined by the holder of power. Pleasing 'the powers that be' becomes the key to an employee's success. The leader is likely to have an autocratic leadership style and the followers will aim to please him or her, rather than focus on doing a good job for customers or fellow members of staff. In a business run as a power culture, the inelegant phrase 'kiss up, kick down' sums up the behaviour of many middle managers. This can affect morale in the lower management ranks.

Role culture

This type of culture tends to exist in well-established organisations with a clear organisational structure and well-defined rules and processes. It means that power depends on title or position in the organisation rather than the qualities or skills of individuals. The following tend to characterise role cultures:
- Focus on mistake avoidance.
- Appropriate for stable competitive environment but not a rapidly changing environment as the bureaucratic nature can make change slow to happen.
- Focus on preserving reputation rather than creating a great reputation.
- Tends to be led by an autocratic or paternalistic leader.

Task culture

This occurs when there is no single source of power but rather power is held by the leader of project teams or task forces. This culture tends to be flexible as it will change with changes in leadership. It is democratic, because it implies that each task will be run by the best person for the job. The fact that different people will be 'the boss' at different times means that everyone can feel that their chance may come. This is likely to lead to high levels of motivation.

However, a problem with a task culture is that sometimes a team may develop its own objectives that are not fully in line with the overall business objectives.

Person culture

This develops when groups of individuals have similar educational backgrounds and form groups to share their knowledge and ideas. It often exists among groups of professional organisations such as teachers, lawyers and accountants. In this situation, staff may each act as individuals, which may mean that outsiders cannot see the culture of the organisation itself.

Application

Remember to look out for signs of culture rather than wait to be told explicitly what the culture is like, as even if it is not a specific question it is a great tool of evaluating other questions. When reading a case study you may consider things such as:

- How open do management seem to staff ideas and feelings?
- To what extent does there appear to be a clear line of division between staff and management? Is there an 'us and them' attitude?
- Does the culture seem positive or negative? Do staff seem to want to be there? Does it seem like a culture that would have a positive or negative effect on motivation, productivity and attitude to quality?
- How does the culture seem to have evolved? In some organisations it comes directly from the top and spreads down. In this case it may be relatively easy to change (especially if new management comes in).

Exam insight

The culture of an organisation is embodied by its staff. When reading a case study you should get an idea of the prevailing culture of the business in question. This understanding will help you to answer all manner of questions, not just those directly related to culture.

For example, if a firm seems to have a role culture where staff avoid making mistakes and thus getting into trouble, this may well affect its decision-making. A firm with such a culture is unlikely to invest in a risky project even if there are huge potential rewards.

Themes for evaluation

Culture is the very essence of an organisation and as such affects all aspects of its performance. As such its importance cannot be overstated. However, because it is a natural phenomena developed over a long period of time it can be very difficult to change and attempts may well be resisted by staff. After all, the culture of the organisation is what staff are used to and what they understand. Changing this may take time and determination.

NOTE: Culture is not what management say it is but rather something that just exists and can be felt by all those involved. Look for evidence of what the culture is like. For example:

- How motivated do staff seem to be?
- How positive are staff about the firm?
- How involved are staff in decision-making?
- How welcome are new ideas?
- Is the culture positive or negative?

Organisational culture is a great evaluation tool. For example, a question might ask whether a firm should invest in project A or project B. After conducting an investment appraisal you may recommend project A. Scope for evaluation might arise by saying that project B fits better with the low-risk culture of the organisation.

Test yourself (20 marks)

1 What is meant by the term 'culture'? (3)
2 Why is culture important? (4)
3 Why may culture be difficult to change? (4)
4 Explain why a role culture may stifle creativity. (4)
5 In which sort of firms do person cultures tend to emerge? (3)
6 State two potential problems with a power culture. (2)

Unit 46 Making strategic decisions

What?

A **strategic decision** is made in a situation of uncertainty and has medium-long term significance for the business. It is a decision that is difficult – impossible, perhaps – to reverse. For example, in 2009 Cadbury turned its Dairy Milk brand into a 'Fairtrade' chocolate bar. This is likely to lead to higher variable costs (paying extra for Fairtrade cocoa) but the Fairtrade symbol on the pack may boost the company's image. Cadbury cannot reverse this decision without receiving dreadful publicity

How?

Strategic thinking involves visualising what you hope to achieve within coming years (given consumer tastes and lifestyles, plus the competition you face), assessing the strengths of your business in relation to those aims, then identifying an approach that can enable you to get there. This process should be carried out with a wide range of senior – and, ideally, some junior – staff in order to get a wide range of views and a real consensus. After this process of strategic thinking takes place, new objectives can be identified and a new strategic plan put into action.

Why?

Day-by-day, managers make decisions that are important in reaching the company's objectives. Most are tactical decisions that can be reversed if they prove unsatisfactory. But Directors always need to be looking ahead to the next 2–5 years. In 2009 JJB Sports decided to sell off the one profitable part of its business (Fitness Centres) in order to concentrate on its struggling sports shops. Big decisions sometimes have to be made, even if they are uncomfortable. Top businesspeople are the ones who can get those decisions right, most of the time.

When?

This is a big question. Many businesses make the right decision, but too late. Later may be no better than never. Kodak kept with camera film for far too long because it was still profitable, but that left the business behind competitors in the new world of the digital camera. Brave managers are willing to sacrifice short-term profit in order to establish a stronger, long-term market position.

Important influences on strategic decision making

1. Relative power of stakeholders

If outside shareholders are all-powerful (as in a plc) the key influence on strategic decision making will be 'shareholder value'. This means the rewards the shareholders are getting from their investment, e.g. how high is the share price? The Directors of the business may feel forced to take decisions that benefit the share price. In 2005 and 2006, banks felt forced to 'go for growth', because that is what stock market investors wanted. The Directors were later to be humiliated by the 'Credit Crunch'.

2. Available resources

Top companies try to make sure that they always have enough cash to be able to put strategic decisions into

Strategic decisions	Tactical decisions
• Should we relocate our factory from Coventry to Cambodia?	• Should we replace our CCTV system as our current pictures are too fuzzy?
• Should we keep opening new stores, even though we're going through a sharp recession?	• Should we mark down the prices on this Christmas stock on December 23rd rather than wait until the January sales?
• Should we focus all our investment capital for the next two years on building a sizeable operation in India?	• Our labour turnover has been rising steadily, so should we conduct a staff questionnaire to find out what's wrong?
• Should we move from Anfield to a new, multimillion, bigger stadium nearby?	• Should we spend £4 million on Porto's bright young winger?

Table 46.1: Examples of strategic and tactical Decisions

practice. At the end of 2009 Apple had $34 billion of cash and cash investments in its balance sheet to provide the liquidity to take advantage of any opportunity. At the same time Ford was negotiating to sell its Volvo car subsidiary to Chinese competitors, just because it needed to raise some cash.

3. Ethical position.

In the 1990s the term 'business ethics' meant little. Today it is a significant part of boardroom discussion in plcs and other businesses. The question remains, however: are the discussions about how to operate ethically, or are they about how to be *thought* to be operating ethically? In other words is it genuine or is it for show? Company directors can be forgiven for being quite cynical about ethics, because consumers are often as hypocritical as companies. People talk about animal welfare but can't resist two chickens for a fiver, and they talk about global warming as they're driving down to the shops.

Approaches to strategic decisions

There are always two alternative methods to making a decision: evidence-based (scientific) or intuition. It is important to realise that either method may be successful or unsuccessful. There is no evidence that one is better than the other.

Scientific – In 2007 senior management at Whitbread plc went through a detailed analysis of the four operating divisions of its business. It decided to sell cash cow David Lloyd Leisure for £925 million, to invest more heavily in rising star Costa Coffee. The strategic decision was based on evidence of the financial performance of the different parts of the business. Therefore it was logical, scientific even. By early 2010 it was clear that the thinking had been sound, as Costa Coffee was growing rapidly, even though rival Starbucks was having to close branches.

Intuition – In 2009, Apple's boss Steve Jobs announced the launch of the 3G iPhone. This was launched without market research and at a time when the first iPhone was still selling well. Apple's hunches have repeatedly been very clever indeed.

The significance of information management

The bosses of most plcs make their decisions on the basis of data, not hunch. Therefore information management is crucial. The first critical issue is to have full knowledge of your own business. This might seem obvious, but in January 2008 a major French bank found that one of its own employees had been gambling with €50 billion of the bank's money. Sorting out the mess cost more than £3,000 million.

Other businesses find out much too late that sales have been worse than expected. Good companies have up-to-date information about themselves. This requires I.T. systems that show instantly how the business is doing, so that the senior directors can think about whether current strategies are working. If they are not, it may be time for a radical re-think.

Evaluation

Strategic thinking should be radical, innovative and free from internal constraints such as 'that's not how we do things round here'. The traditions and culture of an organisation should always be taken into account but cannot be allowed to limit a firm's future. Careful discussion with a wide range of staff should help bring insight to the process and to help communicate the need for a new approach.

A* Insight

Because strategic decisions cannot easily be reversed, it is exceptionally important to consider what might go wrong and how serious the implications might be. The decision to refinance Woolworths through a massive sale-and-leaseback deal resulted in the company's death. When looking at an exam case study, think hard about the company's circumstances. Might the strategic decision prove a disaster?

Key terms

Cannibalisation – 'eating your own kind', i.e. launching new products that will take sales largely from your own brands.
Strategic decision – one that is made in circumstances of uncertainty and where the outcome will have a major impact on the medium-long term future of the organisation.
Tactical decisions – deciding what to do in circumstances that are immediate (short-term) and where a mistake is unlikely to have a major impact on the business.

Test yourself (20 marks)

1 Explain why a strategic decision is hard to reverse. (4)
2 Strategic or tactical? Put an S or a T by each of the following: (4)
   a) BP decides to increase the price of its petrol by 3p a litre.
   b) Primark decides to open a chain of higher-priced 'Primark Elite' shops.
   c) HMV closes all its Waterstone's book shops to only sell books on-line. (3)
3 Identify two reasons for and two against Sainsbury's deciding to launch a new national newspaper. (4)
4 Should business ethics ever be a matter of tactics, or should they always be part of the strategic thinking behind strategic decisions? (5)

Change management is the process of controlling the activities carried out in order to facilitate a change to the organisation.

Why?

It is important that the need for change is identified and shared with staff. If employees understand why the change is necessary they are more likely to support, or at least accept, it. The cause of change may arise from internal or external pressures. Possible causes include:

- changes in objectives and/or strategy (internal)
- changes in the size of the organisation (internal)
- changes in management/ownership (internal)
- changes in consumer attitudes/behaviours (external)
- changes in government legislation (external)
- economic changes (external).

When?

Some changes can be anticipated, for example internal changes will often be planned. Changes in legislation may also be known well in advance, making them easier to prepare for than totally unexpected change.

However some changes, for example, changes in the number/quality/price of a competitive product or an unexpected economic downturn may be hard to anticipate and therefore cannot be planned for.

In 2000 Sainsbury's appointed a new boss. He recognised that Tesco had overtaken Sainsbury's in the efficiency of its distribution systems. So he announced a multibillion pound plan to upgrade Sainsbury's IT systems. After many delays the new system started in 2004 and was quickly recognised as faulty. It resulted in Sainsbury' becoming the leading supermarket for – empty shelves. Soon after, the boss was gone and so was the IT system. More than £1,000 million was wasted on an IT system that was supposed to change things for the better, but made them worse. It was a reminder that the Tesco *kaizen* approach ('Every Little Helps') beats drastic catch-up investment every time.

How?

One of the hardest problems in managing change is coordinating the different activities. If two businesses are to be merged, there are a huge number of practical problems, such as making sure that the IT systems are compatible, and that suppliers are contacted just once, by a single (powerful) buyer. To get everything into place in time for a specific changeover date, network analysis is commonly used. In other words, the managers draw up a huge critical path diagram and then work out the completion date for each stage.

Which?

Barriers to change

- **A culture resistant to change** may make it difficult for management to manage the change effectively.
- **Poor leadership** can mean staff tend either to be opposed to the leadership or ambivalent toward them. In either case employees are less likely to be supportive of changes led by the leadership team.
- **Lack of training.** If staff feel unable to perform new activities due to a lack of training they may become resistant and/or less than supportive.
- **Poor communication.** A lack of communication of the reasons for change and the expected results can lead to a lack of employee understanding of what is happening and why.

Resistance to change

Individuals or groups within the business may actively seek to disrupt change. This has happened in the past at football clubs where the players dislike or mistrust the new manager. In 2009 it happened at the Post Office, with staff unhappy at the attempt to switch postmen from experts (knowing 'their' round) to casual staff. Resistance to change can take two forms:

- **Active**: Industrial action such as an official strike (if the workers are represented by a trade union) or a go-slow.
- **Passive**: This could just be showing a lack of enthusiasm or cooperation or failing to respond to changes.

NOTE: students often assume that if managers attempt to implement a change, staff always follow. In reality numerous changes are attempted and fail. For example, some hugely expensive computer systems or programs are bought with a view to revolutionising the way a business works but many staff just continue to use the old system.

In order to prevent or overcome resistance firms can:

- ensure employees understand why the change is taking place
- ensure employees are aware that this change is actually going to be made and they need to get on board
- senior management need to provide the necessary resources and training.

Managing change

There are two stages to managing change:
1 Control
2 Review

Controlling involves ensuring that the intended changes are actually made in order to achieve their objectives. Control also involves ensuring that the changes are made in the way they are intended and when they are intended. It requires regular checks to make sure the project is on course and that employees are on board in order to avoid unnecessary delays.

Review involves looking back at whether an implemented change succeeded in achieving its objectives. This may lead to analysis of potential future changes in a similar direction (if successful) or lead the management to consider how the change could have been implemented more smoothly (if successful or not).

A* insight

Most A level answers see business as a matter of thinking, planning and analysing. That is true, but not the whole truth. Business success ultimately comes from what you do, not what you think. Change management is a case in point. Good plans can become disasters when in operation – perhaps because the person in charge is too laissez-faire; or because they plough on with the same plan, even when circumstances have changed.

Key terms

Industrial action – workers acting to slow down or stop the production process in order to strengthen their hand in negotiation.

Resistance to change – active or passive behaviour designed to make it hard for the change to succeed – in the hope that it will be postponed or cancelled.

Application

When considering the necessity of change or the ability of leadership to manage change, it is important to look at various aspects of the business in question including:

- the strength of leadership
- the culture of the organisation
- the market position of the organisation.

Themes for evaluation

All organisations have to implement changes on a regular basis. The questions you need to consider are 'How radical are the changes being made?', 'How necessary are the changes?' and 'Is the change worth the problems they may cause?'. Having considered this issue, be prepared to explain your judgement. It may be that you think the right plan is being implemented at the wrong time: say so, then justify your argument.

Another line of evaluation is the consideration of whether the changes being implemented actually fit with the firm's corporate objectives. If not, are they just being made for change's sake? For example, a newly appointed boss may decide to 'put his stamp' on the business through a big reorganisation. If staff suspect the motives for change are personal or careerist, they cannot be blamed for resisting.

Test yourself (24 marks)

1 Why are staff often resistant to change? (3)
2 Outline two potential barriers to change. (4)
3 Outline two strategies for minimising the resistance to change. (4)
4 Explain the terms 'control' or 'review' with respect to managing change. (4)
5 Why may the culture of the organisation effect the management and implementation of change? (5)
6 Explain two reasons why an organisation may need to change. (4)

Implementing and managing change

Answers

Unit 1

Test yourself

1 A corporate objective is a company-wide goal that must be achieved in order for a firm to reach its overall aim.
2 It is not specific, measurable or time-specific.
3 Diversification involves entering an unknown market with a new product. Therefore there is a lot of uncertainty involved, thus increasing the level of risk.
4 Diversification enables a firm to spread risk by reducing the reliance on a particular product or market. The wider the range of products/markets covered by a firm, the less vulnerable they will be to external changes.
5 A corporate strategy is a medium to long-term plan designed to achieve the business's corporate objectives.
6 ● New entrants
  ● Bargaining power with customers
  ● Bargaining power with suppliers
  ● The degree of direct competition
  ● Threat of substitute products

Unit 2

Test yourself

1 A corporate objective is a specific goal whereas an aim is a statement of general intent.
2 A mission statement tends to be written with the purpose of inspiring stakeholders, whereas an aim is purely functional and does not have this purpose.
3 It affects almost every aspect of employee's performance, from productivity to attitude to wastage, quality and customer service.
4 Possible answers include:
  ● The management attitude to risk. If the management is averse to risk, this may result in a culture of caution and mistake avoidance.
  ● The attitude of management. This will be particularly important in small organisations where the owner/manager will tend to be the focal point.

● The aims and objectives of the organisation. An aim of profit maximisation may result in a very different organisational culture than an aim of diversification.
5 In order for these three key aspects to work together and build upon one another rather than cause confusion and division in the organisation.
6 The mission model suggests that the purpose of a mission statement is to bring the four key elements within an organisation (purpose, values, strategy and standards and behaviours) together and ensure they develop in the same direction.

Unit 3

Test yourself

1 To give a department a goal which they must achieve in order for the corporate objective to be met.
2 Often set by the director or senior manager in that function. However, they may have to be agreed with the board of directors.
3 ● To increase sales by 10% by 2011.
  ● To increase repeat purchase to 35% by 2010.
  ● To achieve 25% market share by 2011.
4 ● To increase production by 10% by 2012
  ● To reduce variable cost per unit to £2.50 by 2012
  ● To increase capacity utilisation to 70% by 2012
5 External constraints could include:
  ● Economic
  ● Consumer tastes
  ● Competitor's actions.
  Internal constraints could include:
  ● Financial
  ● Operational
  ● Personnel.
6 In order to plan for how they will be affected. For example, if the marketing department have an objective to increase sales by 10%, the finance department may need to make extra finance available for marketing activity, the operations department may need to increase production and the HR department may need to hire extra staff/train existing staff.

Unit 4

Test yourself

1 The shareholder approach involves a business acting primarily on behalf of its shareholders whereas a stakeholder approach will attempt to satisfy all stakeholder groups in equal measure.

2 It may improve the firm's relationship with stakeholders, thus benefiting the firm in several ways. For example, a better relationship with the local community may reduce negative attention from pressure groups and make recruitment easier. It may also improve the firm's image amongst customers if they are perceived to act on behalf of all stakeholders and accept their social responsibilities.

3 Possible answers include:
- Improves image
- Attracts new segments of the market
- Reduces negative attention from pressure groups
- May differentiate the brand
- May increase sales.

4 Each stakeholder group has its own objectives, some of which will conflict with each other. For example, shareholders may want short-term profits but the local community may want investment in the local area. These two objectives are impossible to satisfy simultaneously in the short-term.

5 As more firms are choosing to act more responsibly this is forcing others to do the same or be perceived as uncaring. Furthermore, in recent times consumers have become more concerned about businesses actions and this is putting pressure on firms to accept their social responsibilities.

Unit 5

Students' own answers.

Unit 6

Test yourself

1 Shareholders, potential investors, banks, employees, managers

2 The purpose of an income statement is to provide stakeholder groups with a detailed breakdown of incomes, expenses and profit made by a firm over a given trading period.

3 Income – cost of sales

4 Gross profit – expenses

5 ● Increasing turnover.
 ● Reducing cost of sales.

6 ● Better control of expenses.
 ● Increasing gross profit at a faster rate than expenses increase.

7 ● In a period of rapid inflation a rise in costs might be inevitable.
 ● If revenue is rising sharply a rise in variable costs will be inevitable.

Unit 7

Test yourself

1 Shareholders, potential investors, banks, employees

2 Fixed assets include: machinery, office equipment, premises, vehicles. Current assets include: stock, debtors, cash, prepayments

3 This measures a business' level of current assets after it has paid its short term debts.

4 Working capital = current assets – current liabilities.

5 Capital employed is the money which has been invested in a business and assets employed is the total value of all the assets a business owns. The value of the assets must be equal to the amount invested in the business.

Unit 8

Test yourself

1 ● It allows for comparisons to be made between firms of different sizes.
 ● It can be used as a measure of performance.
 ● It is useful for analysing the financial performance of a firm.

2 Liquidity refers to the ability of a firm to pay its short-term debts with its current assets. The more liquid the firm, the better the short-term financial health.

3 The acid test ratio is a more cautious measure as it deducts stock from the current asset's value whereas the current ratio includes stock as a current asset.

4 Possible answers include:
- Increase price.
- Reduce fixed costs.
- Reduce variable costs.
- Increase price at a faster rate than costs increase.

5 It implies that the firm are being overly cautious and not ambitious enough in their growth strategy. In good economic times it may well be worth borrowing money in order to increase the size and potential of the business.

Unit 9

Test yourself

1 a) When accounts are so precise to be questionable.
  b) Taking actions that present the published accounts in a better light than would otherwise be the case.
2 Profit does not take into account other vital factors such as management quality, staff loyalty and motivation, strategic planning or commitment to ethics. These factors may be a better indication of future potential profit.
3 Possible answers include:
  ● Bring forward sales to an earlier period.
  ● Change depreciation method to reduce expenses.
  ● Selling off fixed assets to improve liquidity position.
4 It places a legal obligation on companies to provide audited accounts that give a true and fair reflection of the firm's financial position
5 Possible answers include:
  ● The method of valuing fixed assets may be unknown.
  ● The method of valuing stock is also likely to be unknown.
  ● If there has been an attempt to dress the accounts, it may be difficult to realise the true value of the firm.

Unit 10

Test yourself

1 Expansion, start-up, to cope with financial difficulties
2 Retained profit, sale of assets, squeezing working capital
3 Bank loan, overdraft, share capital
4 ● The opportunity cost involved.
  ● How much money is required.
5 ● If a competitor enters the market with a lower price, the business may find themselves forced to reduce price or suffer a substantial fall in demand.
  ● May reduce the quality of good/service.
6 ● Enables the lowest possible price to be charged, thus improving competitiveness.
  ● Or enables higher profit margins to be made.

Unit 11

Test yourself

1 From the following cash flows, calculate which is the better investment, using pay-back and ARR.

	INVESTMENT A		INVESTMENT B	
	Net cash flow	Cumulative cash	Net cash flow	Cumulative cash
Now	(£80,000)	(£80,000)	(£50,000)	(£50,000)
Year 1	£10,000	(£70,000)	£0	(£50,000)
Year 2	£70,000	–	£32,000	(£18,000)
Year 3	£36,000	£36,000	£36,000	£18,000

Pay back: A = 2 years; B = 2 yrs 6 months
ARR: A = 15% (£12,000/£80,000 x 100) B = 12% (£6,000/£50,000 x 100)
So A has a quicker payback and a higher ARR. It's the better of the two.

2 Using payback and ARR, decide whether it should proceed or not?

	Sales	Cash in	Cash out	Net cash	Cumul. cash		
	NOW		–		£400,000	(£400,000)	(£400,000)
Year 1	200,000	£400,000	£300,000	£100,000	(£300,000)		
Year 2	300,000	£600,000	£420,000	£180,000	(£120,000)		
Year 3	150,000	£300,000	£240,000	£60,000	(£60,000)		

On the basis of these forecasts and a three year project life, there is no financial reason to proceed.

Unit 12

Test yourself

1 A marketing objective is a marketing-related goal that must be achieved in order for an organisation to achieve its overall business objective.

2 Possible answers include:
- Enables firm to increase price.
- Reduces price elasticity of demand.
- Increases competitiveness.
- May improve brand loyalty.

3 Increasing sales will only result in increasing market share if the sales are increasing at a faster pace than the market is growing.

4 Answers include:
- Improves branding.
- Increases customer's faith in the product/service.
- May make it easier to succeed with strategies of product or market development.

5 External constraints:
- changes in consumer tastes
- negative publicity thwarting sales growth potential
- competitor's actions.

Internal constraints:
- personnel
- financial
- operational (e.g. in store capacity).

Unit 13

Test yourself

1 Sales promotion may help a firm to increase the awareness and, in turn, sales of a product but has limits in its usefulness, whereas market analysis can steer a firm in the right direction in terms of product development and release, choosing the right strategy for the right external environment and preventing the firm wasting valuable time and resources on duff ideas.

2 Just because there is a gap in the market does not mean that customers desire a product in that gap. For example, there may be a gap in the chocolate market for a high price, low quality chocolate but customers are unlikely to want such a product.

3
- It is based on actual results rather than expected actions of customers.
- Test marketing proves that the product can sell in the market, market research can only suggest it will sell.

4 It may help them to plan for expected income and spending (on materials). This will be useful for preparing budgets and setting targets for staff.

5 Extrapolated figures will only be correct if the market environment remains constant. If there are changes (e.g. economic, consumer behaviour, population changes) the extrapolated figures may prove to be incorrect.

Unit 14

Test yourself

1
- To improve stock control.
- To reduce stock wastage.
- To ensure there is enough stock to cope with demand.
- To ensure the right number of employees are hired.
- For cash flow forecasting purposes.

2 Forecasting future trends based on past data. This can mean extending a line on a graph in its trend direction.

3
- In order to assess the effectiveness of advertising.
- It will assist the firm in forecasting sales.

4 It assumes that it is only one variable affecting another whereas in reality there are numerous variables all affecting one another. Even if correlation between advertising and sales is ordinarily very strong, this might change as competition changes or incomes fall.

Unit 15

Test yourself

1 A carefully considered plan for the marketing activity required in order for the corporate objectives to be met.

2 A strategy has medium to long-term implications whereas a tactic only has short-term implications for a firm.

3 Ansoff's Matrix is used to assess the level of risk involved in pursuing different strategies.

4 a) Penetrating an existing market with an existing product.
   b) Entering a new or different market with an existing product.
   c) A strategy of releasing a new or modified product into a known market.
   d) A strategy which involves releasing a new product into a new market.

Unit 16

Test yourself

1 A document which sets out which marketing activities will be done and when.
2 Answers include:
   ● Outlines clearly which activities will be carried out, when and by whom.
   ● It may help a business to prepare for potential problems.
   ● It should give staff a clear idea of how the marketing activities fit with the overall business objectives.
   ● Can provide a measurement for success.
3 ● Competitor's reactions.
   ● Changes in the external environment forcing the plan to change (e.g. customer tastes and attitudes or the economic climate).
4 ● Financial (whether there is the finance available to cope with the marketing activities outlined in the plan).
   ● Operational (whether there is the production capacity to cope with the extra demand deriving from marketing activities).
   ● Personnel (are the right personnel available to execute the plan?)
5 Analysing the performance of past marketing activities should help the firm to improve marketing decisions in future.

Unit 17

Test yourself

1 Span of control means the number of subordinate workers for whom a manager is responsible. Chain of command refers to the line of authority and communication within a business.
2 A tall organisation has many layers within its hierarchy, whereas a flat organisation has relatively few. This tends to mean that managers in tall organisations have relatively narrow spans of control, whereas managers in flat organisations have much wider spans of control.
3 Reasons include: to reduce labour costs by reducing the number of managers within the business; to improve the speed and quality of communications between those at the top and those at the bottom of the hierarchy.
4 Delayering is likely to increase the responsibility for remaining managers, leading to increased stress and loss of productivity; subordinates may have less contact and direct communication with their managers, reducing the level of supervision and increasing the chances of misunderstanding; fewer layers in the hierarchy may make in more difficult to achieve promotion.
5 Benefits include: frees up senior managers to concentrate on strategic decisions; creates opportunities for more junior staff to develop management skills; increased motivation from giving staff more responsibility.
6 Factors that can influence the success of delegation include: the ability of managers to relinquish some of their control to subordinates; the willingness of junior staff to accept greater responsibility; the availability of finance in order to train managers and workers to deal with delegation effectively.
7 Directors are senior employees who tend to focus on long-term, strategic decisions, whereas more junior managers are usually responsible for organising and controlling short and medium term activities.
8 Causes of falling labour productivity include: a lack of training, failure to invest in modern equipment, loss of worker motivation.
9 Negative consequences include: a loss of worker experience and interruptions to production costs while vacancies remain unfilled; reduced motivation of remaining staff as their workgroups are broken up and their workload increases; increased recruitment and training costs in order to replace staff.
10 A business might choose to recruit new staff in order to replace staff who have left, to increase the size of the workforce in response to an increase in demand, to acquire new skills or experience in order to support the development of new products or markets.
11 External recruitment may be necessary because no internal candidates possess the skills required and it may be quicker and cheaper to recruit staff who already possess the skills required, rather than training existing employees.
12 Benefits include having a more competitive and flexible workforce. Costs include the financial expense and the disruption to production while staff are training.
13 On the job training is less disruptive to production as staff continue to work while updating their skills, but acquiring new skills may take more time as staff cannot concentrate fully on their training.
14 A highly motivated workforce is likely to be more productive, be absent less frequently, more willing to suggest ideas for improvements and take on more responsibilities.
15 According to Herzberg, the presence of hygiene factors, such as satisfactory pay rates and working conditions, does not motivate, but their absence is likely to lead to poor motivation. Genuine motivators, including recognition, greater responsibility and chances of promotion, can motivate employees to work harder.

16 According to Maslow, lower order physiological and security needs must be satisfied before higher order needs, such as esteem and self-actualisation, can be addressed.

17 Fringe benefits are received in addition to wages or salaries and include such things as a company car, discounts on company products, company pension scheme and private medical insurance.

18 Performance-related pay is a bonus payment that is related to an individual employee's work, usually set against a range of pre-set targets. Profit sharing involves paying bonuses by sharing out a percentage of the profit made by a firm, so is based on overall, rather than individual, performance.

19 Methods of job enlargement include: increasing the number of tasks at the same level of difficulty and responsibility; increasing the variety of tasks to include some with greater levels of difficulty and responsibility.

20 Suggestions include: Maslow's social needs; Herzberg's notion of job enrichment; Mayo's belief in the importance of the social environment within the workplace.

Unit 18

Test yourself

1 Two possible areas include the line managers responsible for employees within a particular area or department, or a dedicated human resources department.

2 Influences are likely to include: the state of the economy, e.g. recession could mean a reduction in the size of the workforce to reduce costs; changing technology, meaning that workers skills need to be updated via training.

3 Possible HR objectives for Ryanair are likely to include increased productivity; achieving pre-determined cost targets; increased staff levels to cope with rising passenger numbers.

4 Hard HRM managers see employees as one of many inputs into the production process, generating an unwelcome but necessary cost for the business. Soft HRM managers, on the other hand, see workers as having the potential to add a great deal of value to a business by developing their skills, abilities and interests.

5 Influences include: the leadership style and experiences of its managers; the attitude of its workers and the nature of the activities they are expected to carry out.

Unit 19

Test yourself

1 The purpose of a workforce plan aims to ensure a business has the right number of workers with the right skills and abilities to meet its present and future needs.

2 The components of a workforce plan include: the firm's corporate objectives, an estimate of the likely size and quality of the firm's workforce and its quality in the short, medium and long term; a forecast of the likely future demand for workers, both in terms of numbers and their skills and abilities; a comparison of the current workforce with estimates of future needs, in order to identify any changes required; an examination of the external labour market in the short, medium and long term; recommendations regarding the policies needed to address future human resource needs, including recruitment, training, redeployment and/or redundancy.

3 Internal influences on workforce planning include: a firm's corporate strategies, its marketing and operational strategies and any financial constraints. External influences include: the firm's sales forecasts, conditions in the labour market, developments in technology and changes in legislation.

4 Factors include: costs because, although redundancies may be designed to reduce labour costs, associated costs in the short term, including redundancy payments, may actually increase costs in the short term; redundancies may also damage employer/employee relations, which can reduce motivation and harm productivity; the firm's public image may also be damaged, having a negative effect on sales.

5 Suggested points could consider the need to create the flexibility required to respond to change, but also the difficulties involved in predicting the changes needed. Evaluation could focus on the importance of developing an organisational culture that is receptive to and even keen to embrace the concept of change.

Unit 20

Test yourself

1 Factors influencing the choice of organisation include: size of the business, the firm's products and market, employees' skills and attitudes and the firm's organisational culture.

2 A matrix structure involves putting together temporary teams of employees from different departments with specialist skills to work on specific tasks or projects.

3 Problems include: the owner or original decision-makers may struggle to give up control; junior managers/staff may lack the skills or market knowledge needed to make effective decisions.

4 Advantages include: senior managers have more time to concentrate on strategic decisions, junior staff are able to develop management skills, branches or divisions have more freedom to respond to local conditions. Disadvantages include: a loss of a standard approach, which customers may object to, it may become more difficult to co-ordinate different parts of the business in order to achieve corporate objectives.

5 Benefits include: a reduction in operating costs as a result of losing relatively expensive layers of middle management; faster and more effective vertical communication due to a reduced number of levels in the hierarchy. Drawbacks include: possible demotivation caused by redundancies and increased workloads for remaining staff; possible negative Impact on performance resulting from losing the knowledge and experience of departing staff.

Unit 21

Test yourself

1 Numerical flexibility involves using alternative methods to the traditional approach of employing workers on permanent, full-time contracts, such as temporary contracts, the use of agency staff, sub-contracting and outsourcing. Functional flexibility, on the other hand, is where employees are multi-skilled and able to carry out a variety of tasks, rather than specialising on one particular job or area.

2 Benefits of increasing time flexibility include: firms are able to tailor their operations more effectively to customer needs and increase the level of convenience offered, staff recruitment and motivation may also be improved, while absenteeism and labour turnover may be reduced, boosting productivity and reducing costs.

3 Benefits of outsourcing include: reduction in labour and other costs, access to staff who specialise in a particular

area. Drawbacks include: less control over output, less commitment to the achievement of corporate objectives than from workers from within the firm.

4 Possible consequences include: a reduction in operating costs as less office space is needed to accommodate staff, greater scope for staff working unsociable hours if they can do so from home; possible increase in productivity by removing the distractions that may exist in an office environment; reduction in the ability to supervise staff closely, leading to possible loss of productivity.

5 Possible answers include: reduction in labour costs by being able to match more closely the number of workers employed to the level of demand from customers; improvement in customer service provision; increased staff motivation from being able to have more flexible working arrangements, eg, part-time or term-time contracts; lower commitment levels and increased staff turnover from those on temporary contracts; possible loss of quality from outsourcing certain functions.

Unit 22

Test yourself

1 Reasons why effective internal communications are important include: in order to provide accurate, up-to-date and easily accessible information for decision-making; to co-ordinate different areas of the business, so that employees work towards the same goals; to clarify the roles and tasks that employees should be carrying out; to provide feedback on performance so that it can be repeated or improved; to improve or maintain good relations between managers and workers.

2 Causes of poor communication include: the leadership style of management, where two-way communication is not considered to be important; the attitudes of employees, particularly if conflict and mistrust between employees or their managers may mean that messages are misinterpreted or ignored; language or cultural issues within the business, where differences may lead to misunderstanding.

3 Possible benefits include: negotiations over issues such as changing terms and conditions, including pay, are likely to be carried out more quickly by dealing with a small number of representatives, rather than with individual employees; increased consultation may improve levels of motivation.

4 Conciliation involves using an independent party to attempt to keep the disputing sides talking, in order to sort out differences and reach agreement, but not to give any judgment as to the final outcome. Arbitration uses an independent party to consider the arguments of both sides in a dispute before making a decision, either binding or non-binding, as to the correct outcome.

5 Arguments could examine: the positive impact of employer-relations on motivation and productivity; the disruption to production, increased costs and loss of competitiveness caused by frequent industrial disputes; other influences on business success, such as satisfying customer needs, investment in new technology and product development and cost control. Evaluation could focus on which of these factors is likely to be most significant to an individual firm.

Unit 23

Test yourself

1 Advantages include the ability to employ staff with specialist HR knowledge and skills who can fully devote their time to dealing with HR issues. Disadvantages include the cost of employing staff who do not contribute directly to production, increasing overheads, a possible lack of understanding regarding the specific skills needed by different departments.

2 HR objectives are likely to include: reducing the level of staff in line with falling sales and output; reducing labour costs in line with falling revenues in order to maintain profit levels; maintaining productivity levels by increasing the level of machinery used.

3 Hard HRM involves seeing employees as simply being one of many inputs into the production process, carrying out relatively simple tasks entitled to little, if any, control over decision-making. Soft HRM, on the other hand, views employees as having the potential to add a great deal of value to a business by developing their skills and encouraging them to take more control over their working lives.

4 Influences include: managers' leadership styles, the nature of the work being carried out, the attitude and skills of the workforce.

5 The main components of a workforce plan are: the firm's corporate objectives; an estimate of the likely size and quality of the firm's workforce in the short, medium and long term; a forecast of the likely future demand for workers; a comparison of the current workforce with estimates of future work; an examination of the external labour market in the short, medium and long term; recommendations regarding the policies needed to address future human resource needs, including recruitment, training, redeployment and/or redundancy.

6 Benefits include: ensuring that the correct quantity and quality of employees are in place when they are needed will help to ensure that the right goods or services are produced when customers need them, but avoid the costs of having more staff than required.

7 Internal influences include the firm's corporate, operational and marketing strategies, as well as any financial constraints. External factors include forecasted changes in sales, labour market conditions, developments in technology or changes in legislation.

8 Issues include possible changes on labour costs, including expenditure on training, the impact on industrial relations and on the firm's image.

9 Advantages of having a functional structure include: chains of command and the responsibilities of individual job roles are clearly defined for both workers and managers. Disadvantages include: communication within the business can be slow and of poor quality; the response to changes within the market may be slow.

10 A matrix structure is made up of teams of employees with specialist skills and of different levels of seniority, taken from different departments to work on specific tasks or projects. The teams continue to exist until the project is completed, allowing for a more flexible approach.

11 As a small business starts to grow, key managers may struggle to deal with the volume of decision-making on their own but may remain reluctant to delegate and give up some control. Junior staff may lack the experience and skills required to make decisions and so may be reluctant to take on the responsibility.

12 Reasons why a firm might choose to change its organisational structure include: because of an increase or decrease in size, to improve the effectiveness of internal communications; to improve flexibility in order to respond quickly to change in the market.

13 Possible benefits include: individual restaurants can adapt their menus to reflect the tastes and requirements of local customers; the motivation levels of restaurant managers may increase as a result of greater responsibility; senior managers can focus on developing new strategies to ensure future success. Possible drawbacks include: it may become more difficult to ensure managers across the company are all working to achieve the same objectives; customers may prefer to have a standardised service available in every restaurant.

14 Reasons include: to ensure that staffing levels are sufficient to meet customer demand at all times; to avoid over-staffing and reduce labour costs.

15 Ways in which an on-line retailer could create greater time flexibility include: employing more staff to work during the evening and at weekends when more customers are likely to call; employing staff on zero-hours and annualized hours contracts, so that staff can be bought in to deal with an unexpected increase in demand.

16 Core workers are those who possess knowledge and skills and carry out tasks that are central to the firm's operations, making them difficult to replace. Peripheral workers are either those who carry out general tasks that support the firm's operations, or they may be highly specialist workers whose skills are not required on a constant basis.

17 Benefits resulting from effective communication include: improved decision-making from the provision of accurate, up-to-date and easily accessible information; better co-ordination of different areas of the business; more clearly clarified employee roles and tasks; regular provision of feedback to staff to help motivate them and improve their performance; the establishment of an atmosphere of mutual trust between managers and workers.

18 Ways of attempting to deal with ineffective communication include: training staff to improve communication skills; ensuring that appropriate communications media are available and used by employees; encourage the adoption of management styles that recognise the benefits of two-way communication; review organisational structures to improve communication.

19 Methods include: the negotiation of no-strike agreements with unions in return for improvements in working conditions, which may increase costs but prevent disruption to production; increase in the level of consultation with workers by setting up works councils or quality circles, which could help to improve communication and trust between the two sides but could slow down the process of decision-making.

20 Conciliation aims to bring together disputing parties and keep them talking, in order to sort out differences and reach agreement, but not to give any judgment as to the final outcome. Arbitration uses an independent party to consider the arguments of both sides in a dispute, before making a decision as to the outcome, which can be either binding or non-binding.

Unit 24

Test yourself

1 Typical operational objectives are concerned with cost, volume, quality, time and flexibility, but they could also relate to innovation and environmental issues.

2 Unit costs are calculated by using the following formula – total costs/volume of output.

3 Capacity utilisation is concerned with the extent to which a firm's maximum capacity is actually being used and is calculated using the formula (Actual output/Full capacity output) x 100%.

4 Causes of spare capacity usually relate to overestimating demand, which might lead to acquiring too much capital or recruiting too many workers. Alternatively, it could be caused by an unexpected fall in demand, due to the effects of recession or an increase in competition.

5 Advantages include having down time to service and repair machinery and the spare capacity to deal with unexpected orders; disadvantages include higher unit costs and the risk that workers may become bored and de-motivated by having too little to do.

6 Methods include increase marketing activities to attract more sales or rationalise operations by selling off land and machinery or by reducing the size of the workforce.

7 Production refers to the total output produced by a business; productivity refers to how efficiently resources are used to generate output, i.e., how much output is produced per unit of input.

8 Benefits include access to employees who specialise in a particular area so should have greater expertise and can operate more efficiently, reducing costs; drawbacks include a lack of control over operations and less commitment of the subcontractors to achieving the firm's objectives.

9 Quality might relate to factors such as product features, reliability, durability, delivery times and after sales service.

10 Quality control involves employing specialist inspectors to check output at the end of the production process in order to identify and reject any items that do not meet quality standards. Quality assurance involves training production workers to check quality themselves, in order to avoid mistakes and wastage.

11 Key features include the acceptance that all employees are responsible for achieving high standards of quality, not just production workers; the use of quality circles to generate ideas for improvement; the belief that high quality is about getting things right first time; the importance of service and after-sales service in delivering high levels of quality.

12 Implications include the possible creation of a USP or means of differentiating products from those of competitors, helping to win more sales and increase market share; a reduction in costs from a reduction in wastage and having to deal with fewer customer complaints; a possible increase in worker motivation, resulting from having greater responsibility and participation in decision-making via participation in groups such as quality circles; an increase in training costs as workers need to be given additional skills; possible disruption to production as workers switch from one production system to another, leading to a fall in output, at least in the short-term.

13 British Airways could increase the number of flights to popular destinations, increase the choice with respect to in-flight meals, or reduce the number of delays or cancellations.

14 Benefits of improving customer service include: improved customer retention, reducing promotional expenditure; enhanced reputation, attracting new customers; reduced rates of customer complaints, leading to lower costs of having to deal with them.

15 Ways of monitoring customer service could include: using market research to assess customer satisfaction; the use of mystery shoppers; use of role play and simulation to assess staff during training.

16 Benefits of having good relations with suppliers include: it can make it easier to negotiate lower prices; there may be improved reliability in terms of delivery and quality standards; it may lead to greater flexibility in terms of changes in volume or design.

17 Factors influencing choice include: the price charged, the quality of supplies, flexibility and reliability.

18 Ways that technology can be used to improve stock control include: using databases to record and analyse stock levels; electronic links with suppliers to allow re-orders to occur automatically.

19 Ways that technology can be used to improve communication within a large organisation include: use of email for sending messages between staff in different departments, teleconferencing for meetings between employees in different locations and mobile phones allowing sales staff to contact head office.

20 Issues include: the cost of technology, availability of finance, the extent to which technology would add value, the impact of introducing technology in terms of training, redundancy etc.

Unit 25

Test yourself

1 An operational objective is a specific and detailed production target set by a business. These objectives could relate to producing goods or services that are produced within certain cost limits, achieve a pre-determined standard of quality and are delivered on time.

2 Firms set operational objectives in order to maintain competitiveness and achieve their overall business objectives.

3 Keeping costs down creates opportunities for charging lower prices, allowing a business to compete more effectively, particularly in markets where customers see low prices as a key influence on their decision to buy. Alternatively, reducing costs but maintaining prices charged to customers generates higher levels of profit, which can be used to invest in developing new products to maintain competitiveness.

4 Operational flexibility allows firms to change production volumes quickly and smoothly in response to unexpected changes in demand. It also allows firms to produce goods that are tailored more closely to the needs of their customers, but still enjoy the cost benefits generated by large scale production.

5 Meeting internal quality standards consistently can help eliminate wastage, helping to reduce costs. A reputation for quality within the market can attract new customers, as well as retaining existing ones, allowing a firm to compete successfully against lower cost rivals.

6 Influences on a firm's operational objectives include: the nature of the products produced, the level and nature of demand for the product, the availability of resources used in production and the behaviour of competing firms.

7 Innovation can help firms develop brand new products or make improvements to existing ones so that customer needs are satisfied more effectively. Alternatively, it can be used to develop production processes that are cheaper, faster and create higher quality products.

8 Implications of setting environmental objectives are that products and production systems may need to be changed and different suppliers used, leading to increased costs. However, being perceived as an environmentally friendly firm can attract more customers who may be prepared to pay higher prices. There may also be human resource benefits as both existing and potential employees may prefer to work for an environmentally friendly firm.

Unit 26

Test yourself

1 Economies of scale occur when an increase in the level of production leads to a fall in unit or average costs.

2 Types of economies of scale include: purchasing economies where suppliers offer discounts for bulk-buying; technical economies where the fixed costs of purchasing machinery are spread over higher levels of output, reducing the capital costs per unit; and specialisation where large firms are able to justify employing specialist teams in these different functional areas because of the amount of work generated, leading to improve performance.

3 Diseconomies of scale occur when an increase in the level of production leads to a rise in unit or average costs.

4 Benefits include: the speed of production is likely to increase; mistakes and variations from the product specification are less likely, reducing waste; production runs are less likely to be affected by staff absences. Drawbacks include: the initial cost of investment; the ongoing costs of servicing equipment and updating the technology used; an over-reliance on machinery may lead to a complete halt in production if something goes wrong.

5 Influences include the nature of the product and processes used, the cost and availability of resources, such as appropriately skilled workers, and the cost and availability of finance in order to invest.

Unit 27

Test yourself

1 Invention involves creating a new idea for a product or production process, whereas innovation involves taking a newly-invented idea and turning it into a commercial success.

2 Product innovation leads to brand new goods and services, which, if successful, can give the firm concerned a competitive edge by being the first in the market. Process innovation involves developing new methods of production that can increase efficiency, improve quality and reduce costs.

3 Adopting a strategy of innovation is likely to affect operations because it is the responsibility of the production department to develop the systems, design or acquire the machinery and train employees to manufacture a new product at the volume, quality and cost levels required to make it a commercial success. From a human resources viewpoint, recruitment or training may be required to obtain the skills required to develop ideas, although in many businesses all employees are seen as potential sources of new ideas and are encouraged to contribute their ideas via quality circles, kaizen groups and suggestion schemes. The finance department is required to raise the funds required to support the innovation process, which may take years to generate any significant income stream and, in most cases, will not succeed in producing products that even reach the market. The marketing department has to identify customer needs and opinions and then put together an effective marketing mix to support the product.

4 Potential benefits include a competitive edge against rivals, enhanced reputation and consumer loyalty, reduced production costs and improved quality levels.

5 Factors include the cost of innovation, an inability to raise the finance required and the possibility that competitors will be able to launch their own 'copycat' products before research and development costs can be recouped.

Unit 28

Test yourself

1 A firm may choose to relocate as a result of a decision to expand, requiring larger premises, or because of a need to find more appropriate facilities, for example with lower operating costs or a more up-market image.

2 Influences on relocation include site cost and facilities, proximity to suppliers, customers or appropriately skilled employees, the quality of the infrastructure and the availability of government assistance.

3 Quantitative methods used in relocation include break-even, as well as investment appraisal techniques such as payback and average rate of return.

4 A manufacturing firm may choose to relocate overseas to open up new markets, to benefit from cheaper labour or lower land costs, to reduce transport costs from suppliers or to customers, to overcome the problems caused by exchange rate fluctuations or trade barriers.

5 Off-shoring refers to the practice of transferring part or all of a firm's operations to a cheaper location overseas. These functions are either carried out in facilities owned by the business, or by an entirely separate firm.

6 Reasons include problems caused by language and other cultural differences, the risk of economic and/ or political instability and also the potential damage to public image, especially if the move leads to a loss of UK jobs.

Unit 29

Test yourself

1 Lean production is an approach to operations that aims to minimise all forms of waste, in terms of materials, energy, time and human effort.

2 Reducing the time it takes to get goods or services to customers can give a firm a competitive edge, especially where customers place a high value on speed and convenience. The ability to design new products more quickly increases opportunities to be first to market, allowing the firm to charge premium prices in the absence of any other competition.

3 Critical path analysis (CPA) is a planning technique used to organise all the different activities required to complete a complex project in the shortest possible time.

4 Benefits of CPA include: it reduces the risk of anything being overlooked that could affect the success of the project; it can help to reduce the time taken to get products to customers, creating a competitive advantage over rivals; it can lead to reduced costs and improved capacity utilisation by identifying exactly when resources, such as stocks, labour and equipment, are needed; it allows managers to focus on ensuring that critical activities are completed within deadlines, so that customer deadlines are met. Drawbacks include: the effectiveness of the technique relies on the accuracy of data used but a lack of experience may mean that estimates of the duration of activities, for example, are overly optimistic; successful implemention depends not just on the ability to plan but also on managers' skills in implementing and monitoring these plans, as

well as the availability of resources such as finance and skilled labour; the planning process can make managers become rigid and inflexible, even if more efficient alternatives are thought up.

5 JIT production cuts costs because, by eliminating the need to hold stocks of either raw materials or finished goods, it reduces the need for warehouse staff and insurance. It also means that wastage is reduced, as stock is less likely to deteriorate or become out of date while it is waiting to be used or sold.

6 Good supplier relationships are important for firms using JIT as they are likely to need a great deal of flexibility in terms of the quantity of stocks that are delivered, as well as the speed and timing of deliveries.

7 Benefits of cell production include: increased worker flexibility as they are more likely to be multi-skilled and perform a range of tasks, covering for other workers who may be absent and reducing the chances of production being disrupted; increased worker motivation resulting from working in groups and having a greater variety of tasks to perform, leading to higher productivity and lower wastage.

Unit 30

Test yourself

1 Kaizen is the Japanese term for continuous improvement and is an approach to operations that is based upon the view that firms can always find ways of doing better.

2 The idea of 'one employee, two jobs' relates to the view that workers should be prepared to carry out the tasks assigned to them, but also be prepared to scrutinize their roles, looking for ways to carry them out more effectively.

3 Worker empowerment is important to kaizen because workers need to feel as though they have the authority and responsibility to suggest and make changes within the working environment that will lead to greater efficiency and improved quality.

4 Team-working encourages workers to support each other and share ideas. The expertise of individual workers within the team increases over time as they carry out all of the tasks within their section and acquire more skills.

5 Kaizen can increase motivation levels because it encourages workers to become involved in the decision-making process. If their suggestions for improving quality are adopted, they are likely to work hard to ensure they succeed. Team-working can also boost motivation by addressing workers social needs (Maslow) and giving them greater responsibility and work variety (Herzberg)

6 Managers and workers need to be trained in order for Kaizen to be adopted, which need to be financed. It

may take time for workers to adjust to different working practices, which may lead to a fall in productivity and increased unit costs in the short run.

7 Workers may resent the introduction of changes that disrupt existing working practices and require them to develop new skills. They may also resent being expected to contribute ideas to improve business performance, which they may perceive as being the responsibility of management.

8 Kaizen involves introducing change on a steady but gradual basis, so may not be appropriate if radical change is required quickly. It may also be the case that the pace of improvement slows down over time as easily-solved problems are quickly dealt with but more challenging issues unresolved, resulting in diminishing returns and a loss of enthusiasm.

Unit 31

Test yourself

1 Operational objectives, like all functional objectives, should be designed to support the achievement of overall corporate objectives.

2 Efficiency looks at how effectively a business uses its resource, for example, the level of output produced per worker or the amount of waste generated by production processes.

3 Increased efficiency may mean that a business can increase the volume of production, without increasing the level of resources used, in order to meet increased demand. Alternatively, the same level of output could be produced with fewer resources. In either case, unit costs would be reduced, creating opportunities for increased profits.

4 A large retailer, such as Sainsbury's, could set environmental targets that relate to a reduction in the amount of packaging on products or plastic bags given to customers, an increase in the number of locally sourced products to reduce fuel consumption, an increase in financial support given to suppliers to help them to become more environmentally friendly.

5 Fit for purpose means that a product should perform the functions that it was designed to carry out, not just when it is bought but for a reasonable amount of time into the future.

6 a) Sony Vaio – memory size and power, aesthetic design, quality of sound and graphics.
   b) Domino's Pizza – taste, freshness of ingredients, conformity to menu description and promotional materials, speed of delivery.

7 Economies of scale occur when an increase in output leads to a fall in unit costs.

8 Purchasing economies – where suppliers offer discounts for bulk-buying; technical economies –

where the fixed costs of purchasing machinery are spread over higher levels of output; specialisation – where large firms are able to employ specialist teams in these different functional areas because of the amount of work generated.

9 Diseconomies of scale occur when an increase in output leads to a rise in unit costs.

10 Benefits of becoming more capital intensive include increased speed of production; a reduction in the number of mistakes, reducing wastage levels; production runs are less likely to be affected by staff absences.

11 It may not be able to raise the investment funds necessary; production volumes may not be high enough to justify the expenditure; the technology to replicate labour skills and offer the level of product variation required may not be available.

12 Invention involves creating a new idea for a product or production process, whereas innovation involves taking a newly-invented idea and turning it into a commercial success.

13 Benefits from investing in research and development include greater price flexibility and greater opportunities to use price skimming; increased market power leading to a great deal of control over price and supply; improved reputation which can act as a valuable marketing tool.

14 An established firm might relocate in order to expand production by moving to a larger site; to improve image by moving to a more upmarket area, or to reduce costs by moving to an area where land or labour is cheaper.

15 Quantitative techniques used as part of relocation include: break-even analysis, which shows how many units need to be sold in order generate enough revenue to cover costs, including location costs such as rent and rates; payback calculates the number of months (or years) it takes to generate enough revenue to pay back investment costs; average rate of return, which calculates the average annual profit generated by a project, expressed as a percentage of the sum invested.

16 Qualitative factors include the image of an area, emotional attachments or the opportunity to enjoy a better quality of life.

17 Off-shoring is the practice of transferring part or all of a firm's operations to a cheaper location overseas.

18 Information that can be obtained from a network diagram include the time required to complete each activity (the duration) and the shortest time for the project overall, the correct sequence for the activities, which activities can take place simultaneously, which activities cannot run over without delaying the project overall (critical activities).

19 Lean production is an approach to operations that aims to minimise all forms of waste, in terms of materials, energy, time and human effort, in order to reduce costs.

20 Benefits of time-based management include reducing the time it takes to get goods or services to customers, giving a firm a competitive edge especially where customers place a high value on speed and convenience. The ability to design new products more quickly also creates an opportunity to be first to market, meaning that the firm may be able to charge premium prices until competing firms arrive.

21 Benefits of CPA include: reducing the risk of anything being overlooked that could affect the success of the project; reducing the time taken to get products to customers; reducing costs by identifying exactly when resources are needed; allowing managers to focus on ensuring that critical activities are completed within deadlines. Drawbacks include: inaccurate data may mean that estimates of the duration of activities, for example, are overly optimistic; a lack of managers' skills in implementing and monitoring plans, as well as the availability of resources such as finance and skilled labour, can reduce the effectiveness of the plan; the planning process leads to management inflexibility, even if more efficient alternatives are thought up.

22 Just in time production involves producing to order, rather than holding large quantities of finished goods in stock, and bringing in raw materials and components from suppliers just as they are needed by the production department.

23 Excellent supplier relationships are important for firms using JIT as they are likely to need a great deal of flexibility in terms of the quantity of stocks that are delivered, as well as the speed and timing of deliveries.

24 Kaizen is the Japanese term for continuous improvement – it is an approach to operations that is based upon the view that firms can always find ways of doing better.

25 For Kaizen to be successfully implemented, a culture needs to be created within a firm that encourages workers to accept the concept of 'one worker, two jobs', as well as promoting teamwork and empowerment.

Case study

1 Possible consequences include reductions in unit costs by generating further economies of scale, including purchasing and technical economies, but also the possibility of diseconomies of scale, such as poor communication, co-ordination and deteriorating staff motivation.

2 Answers should focus on the cost savings generated from the reduction in waste, reducing prices charged to customers and helping to achieve funds to finance investment in further innovation.

3 Dell competes in the highly competitive and rapidly changing computer industry. Constant innovation

is required to find new and more effective ways of satisfying customer needs, in order to offer products that match (and, ideally, surpass) those of rival firms.

4 Answers should examine the potential cost benefits of switching locations, as well as the potential advantages of being located closer to new customers or suppliers, in comparison to the potential loss of sales generated by the resulting negative publicity. In the highly competitive IT market, customers are more likely to be influenced by cost.

Unit 32

Test yourself

1 External influences are factors, such as changes in technology or the law, that are beyond the control of a business but that can still affect its performance.

2 An increase in interest rates would make borrowing more expensive for consumers, so may reduce the demand for goods likely to be bought on credit. It would also make borrowing more expensive for businesses, so may discourage taking out loans for investment in expansion. The retailer may also experience a rise in costs and possible cash flow problems if it has a significant overdraft or other existing borrowings subject to interest rate changes.

3 Manufacturers and retailers that produce and sell healthier snacks and drinks may benefit as demand for their products increases and the cost of advertising becomes cheaper; firms such as McDonalds, KFC and Dominos Pizza will need to develop alternative ways of promoting products, such as more special offers, and/or develop more healthy food choices for customers to prevent a fall in demand; advertising agencies and commercial TV channels may need to reduce their rates to attract new customers.

4 Suggestions include: advertise their products on search engines such as Google, as well as their own websites; develop the ease of use of Internet banking and promote the benefits of using such facilities to customers.

5 It may become more difficult to recruit young people to fill part-time and seasonal jobs; it may need to adapt its product range to focus more on the needs of older age groups.

Unit 33

Test yourself

1 a) characteristics of a boom – low levels of unemployment, rates of economic growth above the long-term average, increasing rates of growth in consumer spending and business investment, increasing inflation and interest rates;

b) characteristics of a slump – negative rates of economic growth, high and increasing levels of unemployment, low and possibly negative inflation (deflation) and interest rates, a lack of consumer and business confidence.

2 Benefits include: the rate of labour turnover, pressure for wage increases and likelihood of industrial disputes is likely to fall, recruiting workers is likely to become easier. The main drawback is likely to be falling demand (depending on the nature of the firm's products).

3 Effects of inflation on business include: rising materials and wage costs, which the firm may not be able to pass on to customers; a loss of international competitiveness; increased costs of having to update price lists more frequently; a reduction in the real value of any business debts; an appreciation in the book value of a firm's assets, making it appear more valuable, at least on paper.

4 If the value of the pound depreciates (falls) against the euro, UK exports to France will become cheaper in euro terms. Therefore, if the value of the pound depreciates from £1 = €1.25 to £1 = €1.10, the euro price of a UK export worth £100 will fall from €125 to €110.

5 An appreciation of the £ against the $ would make UK exports to the US more expensive, if $ prices are adjusted to reflect the change. Chase could choose to leave the dollar price Chase could leave $ prices unchanged, particularly if the value of £ was expected to fall again in the near future, but this would cause sterling revenues to fall in the short term. It could allow $ prices to increase, in order to maintain sterling revenues, but this could cause demand to decrease, especially if cheaper substitutes exist. Price sensitivity could be reduced by the use of promotion to build the brand's image.

Unit 34

Test yourself

1 Globalisation refers to the increasing trend for markets to become international in nature, sharing the same characteristics and making it easier for businesses to operate on a worldwide scale.

2 Opportunities include: increased sales from operating in a number of markets, increasing revenues and hopefully generating higher profits; increased economies of scale from operating on a larger scale, particularly if a business is able to produce and sell a standardised product on a global scale; access to cheaper resources, increasing the efficiency of business operations; access to better qualified or skilled employees, with a better understanding of local markets and customer needs,

meaning that products can be designed to match these needs more closely.

3 Possible threats include: competition, particularly from firms based in developing countries where goods can be produced at a lower cost making it difficult, if not impossible, to compete on the basis of price; the threat of takeover from large multi-nationals keen to gain control of successful products and gain fast access to markets worldwide; accusations of exploitation for firms that locate or use suppliers based in low-wage economies, potentially damaging sales.

4 Benefits include opportunities to sell to new markets with huge populations and access to sizeable pools of cheap labour.

5 Possible strategies include: relocate manufacturing to a cheaper location overseas, in order to reduce costs and become more price competitive; focus on producing high quality garments for niche markets, emphasising the 'English' brand.

Unit 35

Test yourself

1 The Government attempts to influence the level of economic activity in order to try to create the conditions required for businesses to perform as effectively as possible.

2 Government macroeconomic objectives include steady economic growth, low levels of unemployment, price stability, a favourable balance on the current account and a stable exchange rate.

3 Expansionary fiscal policy could either include an increase in government spending on areas such as education, health care or benefits. Alternatively, it could involve a reduction in the level of taxation by, for example, reducing the rates of income or corporation tax.

4 Possible benefits include: an increase in demand as consumers use cheaper credit to finance furniture purchases; a reduction in costs as the interest paid on existing debts, such as mortgages and overdrafts, is reduced; access to funds for investment as new borrowing becomes cheaper.

5 Supply side policies include: government legislation to increase labour market flexibility, making it easier for firms to employ, redeploy or dismiss workers in response to changes in demand; increasing the quality of education and training in order to improve workers' skills and make them more productive; increase the incentive to work, increasing the supply of labour and helping to keep wage rates down; privatisation of nationalised industries and deregulation of markets, increasing competition and efficiency.

Unit 36

Test yourself

1 Benefits include: access to a much larger market, leading to potentially higher sales and profits; access to a larger workforce, meaning that vacancies can be filled more quickly and wage rates can be kept down; free movement of capital, making it easier for firms to invest or relocate in other member states.

2 Possible implications include: UK businesses trading with firms in the euro-zone continue to suffer from exchange rate fluctuations, making it difficult to predict costs and/or revenues; comparing the prices of goods supplied by UK and euro-zone firms is more difficult.

3 The World Trade Organisation (WTO) promotes free trade in goods and services by encouraging countries to abolish tariffs and quotas, as well as by dealing with trade disputes that arise. Members must abide by its rulings and trade sanctions can be imposed against those that ignore its decisions.

4 Effects of employment legislation on UK firms include: increased costs created by the existence of the minimum wage and statutory redundancy payments, protection of workers rights regarding areas such as maternity/paternity leave and unfair dismissal.

5 Benefits include: having a reputation for respecting consumer rights, which could help to increase sales and maintain customer loyalty; avoiding prosecution for breaking the law, leading to fines and increased costs.

Unit 37

Test yourself

1 Tactical changes are designed to affect certain aspects of business performance in the short-term. Strategic changes, on the other hand, have bigger impact on overall business performance in the long term.

2 Advantages include: appeal to more customer segments, generating more sales; premium prices charged for more expensive brands may lead to higher profit margins; diversifying reduces dependency on one particular customer segment. Disadvantages include: difficulty in establishing an upmarket brand if the retailer has an established downmarket image; existing customers may also object to attempts to change its image and go elsewhere.

3 Reasons include: to move to larger or more suitable premises; to move nearer to new customers or suppliers; to benefit from cheaper labour or other operating costs.

4 Existing workers are already familiar with the firm's working practices, avoiding the need for induction

training; showing commitment to existing workers may boost motivation and reduce labour turnover; avoid the costs and delays that recruiting new workers might involve.

5 Considerations would include the amount of finance required, availability, cost, level of risk, length of time for which the finance is required.

Unit 38

Test yourself

1 Ethical behaviour involves doing what is morally acceptable, rather than just acting within the law.

2 The shareholder concept refers to the view that managers within a firm should act on behalf of the shareholders of the business, putting their interests and the need to make profit before all other considerations. The stakeholder concept, on the other hand, refers to the view that managers have responsibilities to all of their stakeholders, including employees, customers, suppliers and the wider community.

3 When attempting to adopt a more ethical culture a firm needs firstly to identify and clarify the ethical issues that employees are likely to encounter (possibly by studying the behaviour of other 'ethical' firms); appoint key employees to act as 'champions' and push change through by motivating others; use training to instill corporate ethics on an individual level and ensure that all employees have the knowledge and skills to make the same ethical decisions.

4 An ethical code of practice states a firm's ethical values and outlines the ways in which it should respond whenever its corporate values are challenged.

5 Possible benefits may include: differentiation from competitors could mean the creation of a unique selling point, attracting customers and allowing premium prices to be charged; having a reputation as a caring employer can make recruitment more effective by improving the quality of candidates attracted to vacancies and result in low levels of labour turnover, reducing recruitment and training costs; workers may also respond positively to working for a business that behaves in an ethical manner, increasing motivation and leading to higher levels of productivity. Possible drawbacks include: reduced profits resulting from higher wages and more training for employees, paying higher prices to suppliers and investing in new equipment and processes to reduce damage to the environment; having to turn down highly profitable investment opportunities, if these projects involve behaving in a way that conflicts with a firm's ethical principles; firms with a tradition of democratic management and decentralisation may find it difficult to introduce more ethical policies across the whole organisation, unless there is general support for such a move.

Unit 39

Test yourself

1 Reasons include: improve public image and avoid losing customers; to create an edge over rivals in order to increase market share; to comply with government legislation and avoid prosecution.

2 Issues include: tackling pollution, increasing recycling and supporting sustainable development.

3 An environment audit is an independent check on the environmental impact of a firm's activities, taking into account factors such as pollution emissions, wastage levels and recycling policies.

4 Publishing environmental audits can generate marketing and human resources advantages by creating an honest and caring image for the firm; possible drawbacks include the cost of compiling reports, as well as negative publicity created by a critical report.

5 Implications include: the firm may need to make changes to the materials and production processes used, leading to short-term disruption and increased costs; the possibility of increased sales and stronger brand loyalty if customers approve, allowing any additional costs incurred to be recouped by charging higher prices.

Unit 40

Test yourself

1 Ways include: using computer aided design (CAD) to reduce the time taken to develop new products and identify new ways of producing them more quickly; using computer aided manufacturing (CAM) to carry out more complex tasks previously done by workers; using technological developments such as video-conferencing and email to improve the speed and quality of communications.

2 Ways include: allowing firms to develop brand new products and to modify existing products in order to meet customer needs more effectively; the use of Internet advertising to promote products worldwide and on a 24/7 basis; allowing customers the greater convenience of being able to order goods online.

3 The increasing rate of technological change means that product life cycles are becoming shorter, forcing businesses to invest greater sums in new product development. However, this ever increasing rate also means a shorter length of time to generate the revenues needed to recoup this investment before new, updated products have to be launched.

4 The cost of keeping up with the increasingly faster pace of technological change may be too high for small firms

with limited financial resources; they may also be unable to afford or justify employing staff with the expertise to utilize the latest technologies.

5 Resistance from workers to new technology may arise from fears of job losses, reluctance to retrain or take on new roles and responsibilities.

Unit 41

Test yourself

1 Factors include the number of firms in a market and the degree of market share controlled by individual businesses.

2 A monopoly is a situation where a market is dominated by one large firm.

3 Price cutting by one firm is likely to result in similar price reductions by competitors, so that any success in winning customers in the short-term is unlikely to be sustained in the longer term. Non-price competition, such as advertising to develop strong brand image, is more likely to result in consumer loyalty.

4 Firms can become more dominant by building strong brands that enjoy a great deal of consumer loyalty, even if prices charged are above those of rival products; they can try to reduce the level of competition by using short-term tactics such as predatory pricing.

5 Responses to increased competition might include: price cutting in order to undercut rivals and retain customers, along with cost reductions in order to maintain profit margins; increase product differentiation to make products stand out from rivals by creating a strong brand image, a unique design or improving quality; enter new markets, such as those located overseas, with less competition and offering greater opportunities for sales growth; take over rivals, reducing the degree of competition and increasing market share overnight.

Unit 42

Test yourself

1 Organic growth is usually considered safer because finance is more likely to come from retained profits than borrowing and the firm has time to adjust gradually and adopt an appropriate internal structure. However, organic growth is relatively slow and may mean that it misses out on opportunities to win new sales due to a lack of resources.

2 Reasons include: it is a faster way of achieving growth; integrating with a firm in another market that has already successfully established itself may be less risky.

3 Horizontal integration occurs where two firms at the same stage of production come together, e.g. the takeover of one supermarket by another.

4 Backward vertical integration involves a firm either merging with or taking over a supplier, whereas forward vertical integration involves a firm merging with or taking over a customer.

5 Conglomerate integration occurs when two businesses from completely different industries come together.

6 Reasons include: to deal with diseconomies of scale, such as poor co-ordination or communication; because the expected benefits of integration have failed to materialize; in order to concentrate on those areas that generate the greatest profits; to raise funds from the sale of non-core or less profitable areas.

Unit 43

Test yourself

1 The business cycle refers to regular fluctuations in the rate of growth of an economy over a number of years, passing from boom to recession and slump then back into recovery.

2 Falling inflation rates lead to greater price stability, making it easier for firms to plan ahead and also improving their international competitiveness. Falling inflation may also lead to cuts in the rate of interest, reducing the cost of both existing borrowing and new loans.

3 Likely effects include: a fall in sales as the demand for new cars is income elastic, a fall in the number of industrial disputes as workers become more concerned about losing their jobs; filling any vacancies that do arise is likely to become easier.

4 An appreciation of the pound against the euro makes UK exports more expensive for customers in the euro-zone, which can lead to a fall in demand; imports of goods produced in the euro-zone into the UK become cheaper, leading to a fall in costs for firms importing raw materials but increasing the degree of competition faced by UK firms competing against foreign finished goods.

5 Fiscal policy involves using government expenditure or taxation (or a combination of both) to influence the level of economic activity. Monetary policy influences output and demand by adjusting the amount of money circulating in the economy by using interest rates, controlling the money supply or manipulating the exchange rate.

6 Globalisation refers to the increasing trend for markets to become international in nature, sharing the same characteristics and making it easier for businesses to operate on a worldwide scale rather than concentrating on one country.

7 Possible benefits include: an increased level of sales from operating in a number of markets; increased economies of scale from operating on a larger scale; access to cheaper resources, increasing the efficiency of business operations; access to better qualified or skilled employees with a better understanding of local markets and customer needs.

8 Possible challenges include: increased levels of competition, particularly from firms based in developing countries where goods can be produced at a lower cost; the threat of takeover from large multi-nationals keen to gain control of successful products and gain fast access to markets worldwide; accusations of exploitation for firms that locate or use suppliers based in low-wage economies, potentially damaging sales.

9 An emerging economy is one where living standards and average incomes are currently low but where economic growth rates are high, implying much higher levels of production and demand in the future.

10 Benefits include: opportunities to sell to new markets, creating sales opportunities for a range of consumer goods and services; access to cheap labour, relative to wage rates in established economies, allowing firms to reduce operating costs and become more competitive; access to natural resources, including iron ore, tin, copper and oil used by industry. Drawbacks include: emerging economies tend to be more volatile, more likely to suffer from high rates of inflation and more vulnerable to recession; current consumption levels of most goods and services are likely to be relatively low, limiting the chances of generating significant profits in the short term; the quality of communications and infrastructure may be poor, creating delays and increasing costs; local employees and managers may lack the skills and experience required by large firms operating on an international scale; governments may be hostile to foreign firms and create obstacles, including import restrictions and high taxes, to protect domestic businesses.

11 Benefits include: it should create opportunities for expansion by making it easier to set up stores in new member countries, generating more revenue; it may mean easier access to cheaper food and other supplies; it may make it easier to fill job vacancies in the UK if workers from new member countries migrate to the UK. Drawbacks include: the company may face increased competition from supermarket chains based in the new member country wishing to expand into the UK.

12 Employment legislation acts as a constraint on business activity in a number of ways, including pay and working conditions, dismissal, discrimination, maternity/paternity leave and trade union membership.

13 Possible consequences of ignoring health and safety legislation include fines and negative publicity, which could lead to a loss of sales and recruitment problems.

14 During a recession businesses usually try to reduce costs, wherever possible, in order to protect profits in the face of falling revenues. This may involve running down stock levels, making workers redundant and selling off assets that are not vital to operations.

15 Operational strategies might include: moving production to a low-cost location in order to reduce costs; investing to increase the degree of capital intensity to increase productivity and reduce unit costs. Marketing strategies might include: concentrating on producing exclusive designs; emphasizing the 'Britishness' of the brand in promotion.

16 Business ethics are the moral principles and guidelines that underpin decision-making carried out by firms.

17 Advantages include better quality supplies and more reliable service, making it easier to satisfy customer needs more effectively. Disadvantages may include having to pay higher prices, increasing operating costs, or agreeing to long-term contracts, reducing flexibility to change to new suppliers and secure better deals.

18 Environmental issues facing businesses include reducing pollution levels, increasing the level of recycling and commitment to sustainable development by using renewable resources.

19 Benefits include the positive publicity generated by showing a commitment to improving environmental performance and receiving a good report; drawbacks include any possible costs of either producing the report or implementing any recommendations and the negative publicity from receiving a poor report.

20 Technology can affect operations by using CAD to design better products; by using CAM to improve the speed and quality of manufactured products; by using electronic communications such as email and teleconferencing to increase speed and reduce costs.

21 Reasons include: shareholders may expect a certain return on their investment; profit margins may already be tight and further price reductions may erode any profits currently being made; it may not be possible to reduce costs any further; retained profits are an important source of investment.

22 Internal (or organic) growth involves expansion by generating more sales from existing or new products; external growth involves integration with another firm, either by merger or takeover.

23 Advantages include increased market share and market power, possibilities of generating economies of scale. Disadvantages may result from possible diseconomies of scale, e.g. poor communication and co-ordination, as well as the possible damage to workforce morale if staff are made redundant.

24 Forward vertical integration involves merging or taking over a customer, e.g. a clothes manufacturer may take over a clothes retailer. Backward integration involves merging or taking over a supplier, e.g., the clothes manufacturer may take over a firm that produces materials.

25 Conglomerate integration occurs when a firm takes over or merges with another in an unrelated industry or sector.

Case study

1 a) Gross Domestic Product is the value of an economy's total output over a given period of time;
   b) inflation occurs when there is a sustained rise in the average level of prices within the economy;
   c) the exchange rate is the price of one currency in terms of another.

2 Unemployment is increasing as a result of recession in the UK economy. Unemployment (and the fear of unemployment) means that consumers cut back on expenditure and, faced with falling demand, firms cut back on production and start making redundancies. Firms also cut back on investment, causing the demand for capital goods to fall. The businesses that produce these goods are, therefore, also likely to make workers redundant.

3 Implications include: greater price stability making it easier for firms to plan and possibly leading to an increase in international competitiveness (if inflation is lower than in other major economies); the likelihood of lower interest rates, leading to lower costs and cheaper borrowing for investment; the probability that the economy is still in recession, however, meaning that demand will continue to fall.

4 Implications include: many major overseas markets, including France and Germany have moved into recovery meaning that consumer demand is rising again making it easier to sell products than in the UK, especially for products whose demand is likely to be income elastic; establishing a foothold in European markets is likely to be easier when the value of sterling against the euro is relatively low; diversifying into overseas markets will help to protect the business from future recession; the firm will need to carry out extensive market research to assess consumer tastes in different markets and identify any differences; it will also face competition from other firms targeting growing markets.

Unit 44

Test yourself

1 a) A change in leadership.
   b) A change in production method/capacity.
   Personnel changes
   c) A change in the marketing of these products toward a focus on calories.

2 Benefits:
   ● Employees will feel like they have had a part to play in the change and therefore should react more positively.

● Increased motivation of staff as they feel more important.
● Likely to result in less resistance to change.
● Can get input from employees which may improve management's ability to communicate and facilitate change.
Drawbacks:
● It may take longer as many different opinions will have to be considered.
● If employees are resistant to it to start it may result in change not being made when it is necessary.

3 a) This is suggesting that the future is inevitable and thus cannot be changed.
   b) This puts forward the idea that one cannot merely rely on past data for forecasting but must consider what will happen in the future.

Unit 45

Test yourself

1 Organisational culture is the very essence of an organisation. It includes the accepted norms, behaviours and ethos of the organisation and it is embodied by the people who work within it.

2 It affects almost every aspect of employee's performance from productivity to attitude to wastage, quality and customer service.

3 Culture is something which is built over time and as such also takes time to change. Culture is the accepted way of behaviour which staff get used to and adopt. It may take time for employees to accept new attitudes and behaviour expectations.

4 There is often a tendency to focus on mistake avoidance. This may lead to the stifling of creativity as employees may be reluctant to put forward, progress with new ideas for fear of saying/doing something wrong.

5 Firms where employees have a similar educational background or set of skills.

6 Answers include:
   ● Morale amongst lower-middle management may be low as the focus is on the person at the top.
   ● If the person at the top is wrong it is fairly likely that no-one will be able to approach them about it.
   ● Staff may focus on pleasing the boss rather than developing the best ideas.

Unit 46

Test yourself

1 A strategic decision involves making a decision that will have long-term implications for the business whereas

a tactical decision will only affect the business in the short term.

2
- Whether to outsource production overseas.
- Whether to diversify into a totally new market.
- Whether to release a new product or focus efforts and finance on existing core products.

3
- Whether to hire two part time staff or one full time.
- Whether to do a buy one get one free promotion.
- Whether to start selling Valentine's stock earlier than last year.
- Whether to start the mid-season sale on Saturday or Sunday.

4
- Resources available (people, finance and productive capacity).
- Power of stakeholders.
- Ethical stance of organisation.

5 Strategic decisions are likely to affect the long-term performance of the organisation and thus need to be carefully considered. It is likely that the decision made will affect the firm substantially and for many years to come so the right decision must be made.

Unit 47

Test yourself

1
- They feel insecure about their future in the organisation.

- They worry about not being able to cope with the changes.

2
- A culture resistant to change may make it difficult for management to manage the change effectively.
- Poor leadership.
- Lack of training. If staff feel unable to perform new activities due to a lack of training they may become resistant.
- Poor communication.

3
- Ensure change is effectively communicated to staff.
- Ensure that employees are aware of why the change is taking place.
- Ensure that employees understand how they will be affected and the strategies in place to help them.

4 Controlling involves ensuring that the intended changes are actually made so as to achieve their objectives. Review involves looking back at whether an implemented change succeeded in achieving its objectives.

5 The culture affects the employees attitudes and behaviours and therefore their attitudes to change. A positive working culture is likely to result in more positive attitude to change.

6 Possible answers include:
- changes in size of organisation
- changes in objectives/strategy
- changes in management/leadership
- changes in consumer attitudes
- changes in government legislation
- economic changes.

A2 Revision checklists

Revision Checklist for Unit 3

How prepared are you to tackle these key themes?

	Very well	OK	No
Understand that each business function has objectives that stem from the overall corporate objectives; corporate objectives may be purely financial or may be based on judgement, ethics or a sense of mission			
Examine whether each business function has objectives that fit with each other; and understand how external factors can constrain these objectives			
Understand a simple Income Statement (Profit & Loss Account) and Balance Sheet, recognising the meaning of key terms: working capital, net assets, capital employed, profit quality and profit utilisation			
Identify relevant ratios for tackling different financial issues, e.g. liquidity, profitability, financial efficiency and gearing			
Calculate, analyse and evaluate ROCE, acid test and gearing ratios			
Set the analysis of a firm's accounts into a wider context of its objectives, ethics (eg window dressing) and market conditions			
Calculate and comment on pay back, ARR and NPV results. Assess qualitative issues relevant to the firm's situation			
Combine investment appraisal and accounts by analysing whether a business can afford to invest in the opportunity it has appraised			
Appraise the financial and business-wide purpose of profit centres and ways of raising capital (as a factor in making a decision about strategy)			
Analyse a firm's marketing objectives and assess whether they fit the firm's circumstances; and decide whether the strategy is appropriate			
Use Ansoff's matrix to analyse the risks involved in a strategic marketing decision, such as whether Sainsbury's should open stores in India			
Interpret sales data and trends, including extrapolated data (for forecasting) or correlated data (to help make marketing decisions)			
Build up or interpret a marketing plan, showing a full understanding of setting and spending a marketing budget			
Understand workforce planning as the way in which an HR strategy is put into practice (especially following a key decision)			
Be able to use AS and A2 terms to assess the impact of a change in the organisational structure: delayering, centralisation or a wider span of control			
Understand the causes and effects of: different levels of capacity utilisation; different mixes between capital and labour intensity			
Draw up a network, showing a good understanding of the value and limits of CPA, as applied to different business contexts			
Make and assess location decisions (including centralised versus multi-site), both UK and international, using quantitative and qualitative factors			
Recognise the value of innovation from a company-wide perspective and assess the importance of effective R&D within this process			
Recognise that risky decision making is a key aspect of business, yet often made with imperfect knowledge. A cliché is valid: no risk; no reward			

Revision Checklist for AQA Unit 4

Can you?

	Very well	OK	No
Critically examine mission statements; then assess whether corporate objectives and strategies are equipped to meet the firm's mission/aims			
Aware of the nature of Board level (strategic) decisions and how they are made in relation to the whole firm, not just a department			
Understand that corporate, strategic decisions may or may not have a moral basis, but always have huge, long-term significance			
Understand that firms might claim to focus on shareholders or wider stakeholders, but the proof of their approach is in the actions that they take. Do they talk about stakeholders, but really target shareholders or, like banks, care only about one stakeholder: higher-paid, bonused staff?			
The opportunities and threats from emerging markets, especially new EU members such as Poland, plus the growth prospects in China and India			
The implications of the term globalisation, both for companies and for countries; see the implications for corporate strategy			
Critically examine Corporate Social Responsibility (CSR), to consider whether it is based upon ethics or the desire to polish the corporate image			
Knowledge of the implications for business strategy of economic variables such as interest rates and the exchange rate			
Understand the role and the scope of government activity, regarding economic policy, the framework of the law, and deregulation v intervention			
Understand, and be able to distinguish between, technical change by product and by process, and be able to identify the winners and losers in this process of change			
Be able to analyse different competitive structures, and see the purpose and problems involved in takeovers and mergers			
See why change occurs from within an organisation, and be able to evaluate whether the change is truly needed or is largely the result of personalities and internal politics			
Explain how change may be carried through by means of a deliberate corporate plan, or may be through a planned contingency response to an opportunity or threat			
Assess the role of leaders, both in theory and practice. Analyse different leadership styles to assess the relationship between leadership and culture			
Can grasp the importance of business culture in determining the ethos, the behaviour and success of a business; realise the difficulty of culture change			
Assess the reasons why staff may resist change, to re-examine whether leaders have the moral authority to be pushing through the changes they believe are necessary.			
Good understanding of strategic models such as the Boston Matrix, Ansoff's Matrix and Porter's strategic matrix. Recognise when each one is helpful.			
Understand that major business decisions are difficult because the future is too full of variables for forecasts to be 'right'. Wisdom requires modesty and the knowledge that getting 2 decisions right out of 3 is very good going.			

Index